The Cultural Awakening

A Framework for Leaders Who Navigate Cultural Difference, Build Cross-Cultural Trust, and Lead with Authentic Intelligence

Magdalena Aguinaga

Cultural Intelligence Solutions

Contents

Foreword

There are books you read for information, and there are books that change how you enter a room. The Cultural Awakening is the second kind.

As a Latina in public service, I have spent much of my career navigating spaces where culture is present in every conversation, yet rarely acknowledged in meaningful ways. I have seen firsthand how misunderstanding, often unintentional, can create barriers to opportunity, limit voices, and shape decisions that impact entire communities. I have also witnessed the extraordinary power that emerges when people feel seen, understood, and valued for who they are.

That is why this book matters.

When I first encountered Magdalena Aguinaga's work, I recognized something immediately: this was not theory. This was lived experience. Her voice reflects the reality of so many professionals—especially women, especially Latinas—who have learned to move between worlds, often without a roadmap. From the factory floors of Reynosa to global boardrooms, Magdalena brings forward the lessons many of us have lived but never had the language to articulate.

What she offers in these pages is exactly that language.

Through *The Cultural Lens™*—Root, Read, Bridge, and Rise—Magdalena provides a framework that is both practical and deeply human. It equips leaders not just to manage diversity, but to truly understand it. And in public service, where every decision touches lives across cultures, that understanding is not optional—it is essential.

This book speaks directly to those of us who have ever felt the need to adjust, to translate ourselves, or to question whether we fully belong in the rooms we have worked so hard to enter. It also speaks to those in leadership positions who may not yet realize the weight of their assumptions, or the impact of their perspective.

As a Latina working in male-dominated industries, I spent years believing I had to prove I deserved to be in every room I entered. I measured my worth by how well I could adapt, how hard I could work, and how convincingly I could demonstrate that I belonged at the table. There was a constant, quiet pressure to validate my presence—to earn space that, I now understand, had already been given to me for a reason. Over time, through experience and reflection, I came to a realization that changed everything: I was not invited into those spaces by accident. I was there because of what I already brought—my perspective, my resilience, my cultural lens, and my ability to navigate complexity with both strength and empathy. The value was never something I had to create in those moments; it was something I had carried with me all along. That understanding transformed not only how I saw myself, but how I chose to show up—no longer seeking permission, but owning my place with clarity and confidence.

What I appreciate most about this work is its honesty. It does not ask us to be perfect. It asks us to be aware. To pause. To question. To lead with intention rather than instinct alone.

Many of us were raised with values that shape how we show up in the world—respect, warmth, resilience, and a deep sense of responsibility to others. These are not limitations; they are strengths. Yet too often, we find ourselves in environments that do not recognize them as such. This book reframes that narrative. It reminds us that our cultural identity is not something to be set aside for the sake of professionalism—it is something that can elevate it.

In public service and private industries, leadership is not just about policy and procedures—it is about people. It is about understanding the communities and people we serve, honoring their experiences, and making decisions that reflect that understanding. *The Cultural Awakening* provides a path toward that kind of leadership.

As you read this book, I encourage you to reflect not only on what you will learn—but on how you will lead differently because of it.

Because the future of our communities depends on leaders who are not only capable, but culturally aware, deeply empathetic, and committed to building spaces where everyone has the opportunity to be seen and to rise.

This book does not just describe cultural intelligence. It demonstrates it—in every story, every question, every honest acknowledgment of what it costs to navigate spaces that were not built for you. Read it. Then lead differently.

Dr. Jennifer Mendoza Culbertson

A Note to the Reader

The stories in this book are true.

They are drawn from twenty-five years of professional life navigating US, Mexican, and Japanese business cultures—from the factory floors of Reynosa and the boardrooms of Indiana to the master's program in Grenoble and the hallways of New York. Every lesson in this book was learned from experience, not from a textbook. Every emotion described was real.

Out of respect for the privacy of the people whose lives intersect with mine, I have changed the names of colleagues, managers, and professional contacts throughout. David, Roberto, and Tanaka-san are not their real names. Other individuals who appear in professional contexts have similarly been given pseudonyms or identifying details have been altered. The cultural lessons embedded in each of their stories, however, are unchanged—because the point was never who the people were, but what the moments taught.

The people I identify by their real names—my father, my mother, Mami Mary, my son Mikel, my friend Roxana, Alejandro, and Cristina Solis Wilson—have each, in their own way, given me permission through the years of trust and conversation we have shared. They are named because their stories deserve to be honored, not hidden.

One chapter references a scholarship essay written by a student from an HWNT-RGV program session. Her story is included with permission, and her identity has been protected. She knows who she is. I hope she knows what her words gave me.

Some of the professional scenarios in the Rise section—particularly those involving organizational initiatives—are drawn from a composite of experiences observed across multiple environments and years, rather than from a single event. This is a common and legitimate practice in memoir, used to protect confidentiality while honoring the truth of a pattern. Where I have done this, the pattern is real even when the specifics have been synthesized.

A note on Cultural Intelligence: The Cultural Lens™ is my practitioner's framework—built from lived experience, informed by the academic field of cultural intelligence research, and designed to be immediately usable in the professional contexts most of us actually inhabit. For readers who want to go deeper into the research foundations of this field, I point you toward the work of Geert Hofstede, Erin Meyer, and David Livermore, whose scholarship has shaped how the world thinks about cultural difference in professional life. This book stands alongside their work, not in place of it.

A note on the framework itself: The stories in this book move between four cultures—Mexican, American, French, and Japanese—because those are the four I have lived and worked inside personally. The Cultural Lens™ was built from that specific experience. But the framework is not limited to those cultures, and it was never intended to be. Root, Read, Bridge, and Rise are four practices that apply wherever human beings from different cultural backgrounds encounter each other—which is to say, everywhere. Whether you are navigating a team across six countries or a single relationship across one cultural difference, the questions are the same. Whose lens am I looking through? What am I missing because of it? How do I connect without disappearing? And what kind of room am I building for the people who come after me? The specific cultures I describe are the vehicle. The framework is the destination. I hope you find it useful wherever you are navigating.

Finally: this book is written in English. Its stories travel between Spanish, French, and Japanese. Some things were said, felt, and lived in languages other than the one you are reading now. Where translation choices were required, I have chosen the words that honor the spirit of the original moment rather than its literal transcript.

Read generously. The world we are navigating together deserves it.

Magdalena Aguinaga

Mission, Texas

Acknowledgments

This book began in a conference room in Reynosa, with four words on a piece of paper and a year of my salary quietly disappearing. I did not know it then. But looking back, I understand that everything I have learned—every story in these pages, every pillar of The Cultural Lens™, every conversation that became a chapter—traces its beginning to that moment.

So I start where the book starts: with gratitude for the experience that made me ask the questions this work is built to answer.

To my father—the first CQ mentor I ever had, before either of us had a name for it. You left Torreón at twenty with nothing but technical training, steady hands, and the willingness to say yes to things that frightened you. You studied English at the kitchen table at night so your children could have more doors. I have spent my career walking through the ones you opened. This book is yours as much as it is mine.

To my mother—María Magdalena, the woman whose name I carry and whose example I am still learning from. You learned French in secret so I would never feel unreachable. You reversed your diabetes with discipline alone. You talk to me every day and my days feel incomplete when we don't. You are the cornerstone. You always have been.

To Mami Mary—mi abuelita. Taken at fourteen, given no choices, and still the most generous woman I have ever known. You got your diploma. You got your doll. You told me to leave when the world expected you to tell me to stay. I am independent because of you. I am educated because of you. I carry your photograph everywhere I have ever lived. I know you are still watching.

To Mikel—my son, my greatest work, entirely his own. You were six years old when you looked at me and said: okay, but you have to do it too. You have been right about most things since. I hope when you are standing in a kitchen in Paris, some Sunday morning in Mission comes back to you. Not as a lesson. Just as a feeling. I love you more than any sentence in any language I speak.

To my brother—younger than me in years and wiser than me in ways I am still counting. You migrated to Michigan, where the cultural contrasts run as deep as anywhere on this continent, and you navigated that distance with the kind of ease that looks effortless from the outside and I know is anything but. You have worked across North America, Mexico, and Russia for a multinational corporation and somehow remained the kindest, most patient person in any room you walk into. You are the best father your children could have—steady and present through every season of their lives. You have been a cornerstone for Mikel in the particular way that only you could be, showing up without being asked and staying without needing recognition. I am proud to be your sister. I am grateful every day that you are in our lives.

◆

To Roxana—who stayed in France and built a life that was always going to belong everywhere. You set the alarm that first morning in Grenoble.

You led. You are the living proof of every Bridge lesson in this book, practiced quietly and thoroughly across a lifetime. You will be among the first guest on my podcast because the wisdom you carry deserves to be named.

To Alejandro—who drove fourteen hours and arrived at my door without calling first. You became Mikel's compadre before either of you knew what that meant. You taught me something in that lecture hall in Grenoble without knowing you were teaching me anything. You are my friend, genuinely and lastingly, in the way that only people from shared foreign experiences can be. I sincerely hope you are joking about Paris. I am fairly certain you are not.

To Norma—my best friend and Mikel's godmother. You are the reason that life far from family never felt like absence. Your steady presence, your kindness, and your unwavering support have made Mission feel like home in the fullest sense of the word. You are strong, determined, and successful in everything you put your hands to—and you are raising Santiago and Sebastian in this same multicultural border world with the same values you have always lived by. Thank you for being our family here.

To Cristina Solis Wilson—Command Sergeant Major, author, strategist, and the woman who opened a Cub Scout chapter for Mikel because two boys needed one and she was the person who could make it happen and now days you continue to lead him with Crossroads and many others just like him. You hold me to a standard I am grateful for. You and Mike are our local family. This work is better because you are in my life.

To my M3 Mastermind sisters. To Giselle, who saw what this community could be before the rest of us knew to want it; Eliza, for your faith and whose consistency makes everyone around her reconsider their excuses; Caro, who gives feedback with the precision of someone who respects you too much to be soft about it; Queen Esther, who brings clarity where the rest of us sit in the fog and who has been my shoulder to cry on with just the right words every time; and Marie, who holds space for the emotional truth of the work in a way that keeps us all honest. Five AM on Wednesdays is a gift. So each and every one of you.

To Eliza Garza and Mija Media House—for believing in this book before it was a book, for and for being a sister in God and in craft. This manuscript reached you because you built something real for Latina voices. Thank you for building it; thank you for your guidance and for believing in more for us all.

To the HWNT-RGV chapter and the Hispanic Women's Network of Texas—for the community, the platform, and the sessions that produced the scholarship essays that produced Chapter Thirteen. To the student who went home and said te quiero mucho to her grandmother for the first time in Spanish: you gave me proof, at exactly the moment I needed it, that this work is real.

To Perla and the Latina Empire community—the women across seventeen cities and three countries who show up before the world is awake to do the work of becoming who they were always meant to be. You are in these pages even where your names are not.

To Sabrina—for every hour work done behind the scenes, for the willingness to learn alongside me, and for being twenty-three years old and already understanding that the work matters.

To the companies that have allowed me to learn and grown while performing my job. Special thanks to Mr. Lattao, your guidance and mentorship are the unwavering legacy you leave to all of us.

And to many more friends and colleagues pages will not be enough to mention by name but you know who you are.

◆

To every professional who has ever walked into a room and wondered whether they were allowed to be fully themselves in it—this book is for you. You were always allowed. You just needed the lens.

And to every leader who has ever been David—who acted from the only framework they had been given, without knowing there was another one available—this book is for you too. It is not too late. The lens is here. Use it.

◆

Con todo mi cariño y gratitud.

Magdalena Aguinaga

The CQ Coach

Mission, Texas

A Blessing Spoken Over the Reader

"Whatever you do, work at it with all your heart, as working for the Lord, not for human masters."—Colossians 3:23

Father, before this reader turns another page, I want to lift them up to You.

You knew they would find this book.

You knew the weight they have been carrying, the rooms they had been navigating, the questions they have been asking quietly when no one else was listening. You see them. You have always seen them. Thank you for the gift You placed in Magdalena—the eyes to see, the years to learn, the obedience to write it down. Thank You for using her story so that someone else's story can find its language. That is what You do. You take what we have walked through, and You make it bread for someone else's table.

Father, bless this reader. Bless the work of their hands. Bless the room they are about to walk back into. Remind them that their profession is not separate from their calling; that what You have entrusted them with, in the workplace and in the marketplace and in the meeting and in the home, is holy ground. They are Your ministers, dressed for work. Let them serve like it.And Lord, remind them—gently, clearly, in the deepest part of where they listen—that they have come into their position, into their room, into their seat at this table, for such a time as this. Not by accident. Not by coincidence. By Your hand and for Your purpose.

Cover this book, Lord. Let every page carry Your Spirit. Let it land where it needs to land, awaken what needs to be awakened, and call forth what You have already placed inside the one reading it.

To You be all the glory.In the name of Jesus. Amen.

Dr. Esther Akindayomi JacksonCEO & Founder, Soul Touch Ministries

Introduction

She Kisses Too Much

David flew to Reynosa for my annual review. He had written four words on my official evaluation: She kisses too much.

I remember staring at the paper, convinced I had misunderstood. Not because the words were unclear—but because they made no sense in the world I knew.

The plant in Reynosa was alive that morning the way it always was. The machinery hummed its steady rhythm. The air smelled of metal and fresh paint. My colleagues moved through their routines with the comfortable ease of people who had worked alongside each other for years—quick greetings, shared jokes, the small rituals that hold a team together.

I had built something real there. I was young, ambitious, and deeply committed to doing things right. I showed up early, worked hard, and took pride in being someone others could count on. My environment was layered with intensity—my direct manager was a Japanese American man, brilliant and disciplined, known across the company for his exacting standards. Through resilience and time, I had earned his respect. What began as intimidation became mentorship. And eventually, even friendship.

Then the company hired a new supervisor. David. A white American man based in Indiana—organized, methodical, stepping into a leadership role for the first time. He would be responsible for managing me remotely, from a corporate office thousands of miles away, while I worked daily on the factory floor in Reynosa.

Different worlds. Different rhythms. Different assumptions.

When David told me he would be flying to Reynosa to conduct my review in person, I felt a mixture of anticipation and nerves. In the United States, I had learned, annual reviews are formal events—structured, documented, measured moments where performance is evaluated and compensation is decided. I understood the basics: this mattered.

But what unsettled me was that he had asked HR to be present.

Even Roberto, our HR manager—a calm and steady man who was rarely rattled by anything—raised an eyebrow when I told him. "Is everything okay?" he asked, genuine puzzlement on his face. I didn't have an answer. I just felt a knot tighten in my stomach.

When the meeting started, everything felt normal—at first. David sat across from me in the small glass-walled conference room, the noise of the factory muffled behind us. He began by listing my strengths. My performance. My contributions. My work ethic. He acknowledged my contribution to improving inventory management, my cost negotiations skills and my ability to build relationships across the floor. Relief washed over me. I felt seen. Validated.

And then his tone shifted. "There's just one issue," he said.

He paused. Looked down at the document in front of him. Then, with a deliberate motion, he slid it across the table.

That's when I read it.

She kisses too much.

Silence filled the room—thick and suffocating. I looked at him. Then at Roberto. Then back at the paper. Neither of us seemed to understand what he was referring to. I could not think of a single moment when I had kissed anyone at work, much less in front of him.

Roberto was the first to speak.

"What do you mean?" he asked, his brow furrowed. "She kisses too much?"

David clarified. It was the kisses on the cheek—the ones I exchanged every morning with my colleagues, my coworkers, my suppliers, my superiors. The greeting I gave to anyone who walked through the door.

Suddenly, it all made sense. And none of it made sense at all.

Because in my world—in Reynosa, in Mexico, as it is across much of Latin America—a kiss on the cheek is not romantic. It is not suggestive. It is not unprofessional.

It is respect. It is warmth. It is connection.

It is how you say: I see you. I acknowledge you. You matter.

Every morning, I greeted my colleagues that way—men and women alike, coworkers and suppliers and visitors. It was natural. Automatic. Completely appropriate within our cultural context. It was, in every sense I had ever known, the right thing to do.

But David had been watching from a different cultural lens entirely. He interpreted it as flirting. As crossing a boundary. As behavior that reflected poorly on him as my supervisor representing an American team.

Roberto stepped in, his voice calm and steady. "In our culture, this is normal. It's a standard professional greeting." A quiet reassurance moved through me. Surely, once this was explained, the misunderstanding would dissolve.

But David didn't change his position. He listened—and didn't shift. "That may be true," he said, "but my concern still stands."

And just like that, those four words remained on my official evaluation. Etched in ink.

Permanent. Documented.

Judged.

I left the room and called my best friend with tears in my eyes.

That year, as I watched my colleagues celebrate salary increases, I stood on the sidelines. I did not receive mine—not because of my performance, but because of a cultural misunderstanding that was never truly understood.

My direct manager, the one who had once intimidated me, actually understood. He saw the situation for what it was. But by then, the damage had already been done. The decision had been made. The record had been written.

And something in me shifted that day. Not in a dramatic, loud way. Quietly. Deeply.

I began to understand that success in a multicultural environment was not simply about working hard or doing things right. It was about something more nuanced than that—more invisible, more essential. It was about being understood. And more importantly, it was about understanding others before they misunderstood you.

That moment—painful, confusing, and unfair as it felt—became one of the most defining experiences of my life. Because it forced me to ask questions I had never considered before: What is "professionalism"?

Who defines it?

And what happens when two definitions collide?

I didn't have the language for it then. But today, I do.

◆

With time, I learned to see David differently. He was not a bad man. He was not malicious, nor intentionally unfair. He was, simply, culturally uninformed. He interpreted the world through the only lens he had ever known—and no one had ever challenged him to look through a different one. No one had given him the tools, the language, or the awareness to pause and ask a different question.

And in that absence, he made a decision that impacted my career and shaped my path.

This is the guide I wish someone had placed on that table—for both of us.

◆

Because what I didn't have then—but what I carry with me now—is a single question that has the power to change everything: Is this bias? Is this fear? Or is this my cultural subconscious—and am I willing to see past it?

That question is what this book will teach you to ask. In every room. Before you react. Before you judge. Before four words end up in someone's official record.

◆

This book is for the Magdalenas—the ones who have been misread in rooms that should have seen them clearly. And it is for the Davids—the ones who were never taught to look.

Both of you deserve better than what happened in that room in Reynosa. This is how we build something different.

◆

ROOT

"You have to know where you come from to know where you are going."

— Maya Angelou

Chapter One

What Nobody Taught Us About Culture

Have you ever opened your mouth—and your mom came out?

You are in a meeting. You are trying to sound composed and professional and entirely in command of the situation. And then, from somewhere deep in your chest, a phrase arrives that belongs not to the conference room you are sitting in but to a kitchen you grew up in, to a woman who smelled like vanilla and determination and who never once doubted that you were going to be something. You hear yourself and you think: not now. Not here.

That is culture. It lives in your voice, in your instincts, in the way you greet people and the way you read silence and the things you assume are universal that are, in fact, entirely particular to you. It arrived before you had any say in the matter. It shaped you in ways you are still discovering. And for most of your professional life, nobody taught you what to do with it.

Nobody taught me, either.

I navigated boardrooms in three countries. I negotiated supply chain contracts in three languages. I sat in rooms full of Japanese executives and American executives and Mexican colleagues and German auditors, reading cultural signals and adjusting in real time, building trust across chasms of difference, and doing all of it by instinct—because nobody had ever given me a framework for what I was doing.

And nobody taught David, the manager who wrote four words on my evaluation that cost me a year of my career.

And nobody taught the executives in Indiana who watched my name appear on a screen and saw only one more among them, not what I had spent years building.

We all moved through a world full of cultural difference with no map, no language, and no tools—just the assumptions we had inherited and the instincts we had developed, for better or worse, along the way.

This book is the map I wish someone had given all of us.

Let me tell you what Cultural Intelligence is—and more importantly, what it is not.

It is not sensitivity training. It is not a seminar where you sit in a circle and learn facts about countries you have never visited. It is not a checklist of customs to memorize before an international trip, or a set of rules for avoiding offense, or a performance of openness that disappears the moment the workshop ends.

And it is definitely not asking you to become someone else.

Cultural Intelligence—CQ—is the ability to see the lens you are already looking through. And then choose what to do with what you see.

That distinction matters more than almost anything else in this book, so I want to stay with it for a moment.

Every single one of us carries a cultural lens. It was ground and shaped by the family we were born into, the language we first learned to think in, the country we grew up in, the generation we belong to, the faith we were raised inside, the neighborhood and the kitchen table and the particular rhythms of the life we lived before we had any say in what that life looked like. That lens determines what feels normal, what feels rude, what feels respectful, what feels like a threat, what feels like warmth. It shapes every judgment we make—and most of the time, we do not know it is there.

We think we are seeing reality. We are seeing our culture.

Cultural Intelligence begins the moment you understand that difference. And it deepens every time you are willing to ask the question that sits at the center of this entire book: Is this bias? Is this fear?

Or is this my cultural subconscious—and am I willing to see past it?

That question changed everything for me. It is the question David never knew to ask. It is the question I wish I had been able to hand him across that conference table in Reynosa, along with a explanation of what a cheek kiss actually means.

It is the question this book teaches you to ask. In every room. Before you react. Before you judge. Before something irreversible gets written down.

◆

Over the years—through the boardrooms and the hallways and the negotiations and the misunderstandings and the moments of unexpected, grace-filled connection—I developed a framework for how cultural intelligence actually works in practice. Not as theory. As something lived.

I call it The Cultural Lens™. It has four pillars. And I want to introduce them to you now, not as a list, but as a journey—because that is what they are.

Root — Before you can understand anyone else's culture, you have to understand your own. Not defensively, and not with pride or shame—but clearly. What did the culture you were born into teach you about authority, about time, about silence, about what it means to belong? What strengths did it give you before you had any choice in the matter? Root is the practice of knowing what you carry, so it stops carrying you.

Read — Once you know your own lens, you can begin to look through other people's lenses with curiosity instead of judgment. Read is the skill of observing cultural signals in real time—the silence that is not disengagement but deep thought, the deference that is not weakness but respect, the directness that is not aggression but trust—and interpreting them through the other person's frame, not your own. This is where unconscious bias gets interrupted. This is where David could have changed everything.

Bridge — Bridge is the active, intentional practice of meeting people across the cultural gap—adapting your communication, your approach, your pace—while remaining unmistakably yourself. There is a difference between adapting and disappearing, between flexibility and erasure. Bridge teaches you to hold both things at once: to meet people where they are, and to keep both feet on your own shore while you do it.

Rise — Rise is where personal awareness becomes collective leadership. Once you know what you carry, can read any room, and can connect across difference without losing yourself—you build environments where other people can do the same. Rise is the legacy pillar. It is not about being at the top. It is about lifting the ceiling so the person behind you does not have to fight as hard to get through it.

Four pillars. One journey. And—this is the part that took me years to understand — they always move in this order. You cannot read clearly until you have rooted. You cannot bridge without knowing how to read. And you cannot genuinely help others rise until you have done all three.

Each of the following chapters is built around one of these pillars, anchored in a real story from my life—or from the lives of the people who shaped me. You will meet my father, who practiced cultural intelligence in a Chrysler plant in Mexico City before either of us had a name for it. You will sit with me in a conference room in Indiana, watching my name appear on a screen and making a choice I would spend years untangling. You will stand in a hallway in New York with a glass door held open, feeling the weight of everything I had quietly given away. And you will read a scholarship essay written by a seventeen-year-old girl who went home after one of my sessions and said, for the first time in her life, something in her grandmother's language.

These are not case studies. They are the chapters of a real life—mine, and the lives of everyone I have learned from and learned alongside. What I hope is that somewhere in them, you will recognize yourself.

✦

Before we go any further, I want to say one thing clearly.

This book is not going to ask you to become someone else. It is not going to ask you to master a culture that is not yours, or to erase the one that is. It is not going to tell you that your background is a problem to be solved or a liability to be managed.

It is going to ask you to look at yourself honestly. To sit with the question of what your culture taught you—what it gave you, and what assumptions it handed you that you have been carrying as though they were facts. That is the only place this journey can start. Not with the person across the table from you. With the one you brought into the room.

My father understood that instinctively. He just never had a word for it. Turn the page, and I will introduce you to him.

✦

A TOOL TO TAKE WITH YOU

Before you begin the next chapter, take two minutes with this question: What is one thing your culture taught you that you have never questioned?

Not something you disagree with—just something you have always assumed was simply the way things are. Something about time, or authority, or how disagreement should sound, or what respect looks like, or who speaks first in a room.

Write it down. One sentence.

You do not need to analyze it yet. Just notice it. That noticing is the beginning of Root.

And Root is where everything starts.

Chapter Two

He Left at Twenty

Growing up, I didn't know the term Cultural Intelligence. But I lived it—through the quiet strength and bold decisions of my father.

He was born in the 1950s in Torreón, a city in the northern desert of Mexico where the sun comes in hard and flat and the streets smell of dust and diesel and the particular ambition of people who know they are on the edge of somewhere bigger. My father came from humble beginnings—the kind of beginnings where you don't spend much time talking about what you don't have, because there is too much work to be done with what you do.

What he had was this: technical training, a steady pair of hands, and a willingness to say yes to things that frightened him.

When the opportunity came to work as a quality technician at the Chrysler plant in Lago Alberto—in Mexico City, hours from everything familiar—he said yes. He left behind his family, his community, the particular rhythms of a life he knew, and stepped into the unknown.

He was barely out of his teens.

◆

I think about that sometimes. The specific courage it takes to be young and leave — not because you are running from something, but because you have decided, quietly and without fanfare, that the life waiting for you somewhere else is worth the cost of getting there.

He did not have a mentor who told him how to navigate a new city, a new company, a workplace full of people from different regions and backgrounds and ways of doing things. He figured it out the way his generation figured most things out: by watching carefully, by making mistakes quietly, by building trust one small act at a time.

He made friends at that plant who would remain friends for the rest of his life. Not acquaintances—friends. The kind that show up when things go wrong, that remember your children's names, that call you on a Tuesday for no reason other than to hear your voice. He built those relationships across backgrounds and temperaments and generations, and he did it without ever reading a book about how to do it.

He just knew how people worked. And he paid attention.

When I was eight years old, Chrysler launched a new engine plant in Saltillo, and our family moved north.

Saltillo sits at a different altitude than the center of the country—cooler, drier, its like a slightly sharper shade of white. It felt different from the first day when we arrived. The people spoke differently, their accents carrying a directness that could sound harsh to ears accustomed to the softer, more melodic intonation of central Mexico. They ate more meat. They observed different customs. Día de los Muertos was quieter there. Día de Reyes barely registered.

It was a difficult move, especially for my mother, who had left her own family and community behind and found herself building a life from scratch in a city that felt, at first, like someone else's. Without relatives nearby, we grew up relying on something more portable than geography: our family values, our warmth, our willingness to find the good in the people around us.

And there good was here. The people of Saltillo were honest and hard-working and sincere in a way that, once you learned their language—not Spanish, but the specific cultural language of that region, its particular rhythms of trust and loyalty—revealed itself as its own kind of warmth. My father's colleagues at the Chrysler plant became our local family. They were the ones who showed up. Who knew our names. Who taught us, without ever saying so directly, that you can make a home anywhere if you are willing to actually look at the people in front of you.

I learned that at eight years old, in Saltillo, watching my father do it.

I remember him at the kitchen table at night, after dinner, with his English textbook open and a small notebook beside it where he wrote vocabulary words in columns. He studied the way he did everything—methodically, without complaint, with the particular focus of someone who has decided that a thing is worth doing and is therefore doing it.

He was preparing for training trips to Detroit. For meetings with American engineers and executives who would expect him to operate in their language, in their professional world, on their terms. He understood that speaking English wasn't about losing himself. It wasn't about becoming something other than a man from Torreón who had made his life in Saltillo. It was about opening doors — for himself, and eventually, for my brother and me. He made sure we had those doors too.

◆

My father taught me—not through lectures, but through the accumulation of daily example—that cultural intelligence isn't about erasing who you are. It's about expanding who you can connect with.

That lesson lived in the kitchen table English sessions. In the way he greeted his Saltillo colleagues, learning the texture of their humor, adjusting his warmth to match the registers they responded to. In the patience he showed in rooms where he was the outsider, yet he maintained confident anyway, because he knew what he brought to those rooms was real.

He traveled across borders for opportunity. I help leaders navigate across cultures for impact.

The parallel is not coincidence. And it is not lost on me.

That is why, when I started the Cultural Decode podcast, I knew who had to be the first guest. Not a CEO. Not a published academic. My father—because wisdom like his, the kind that was never written down or formally recognized, is exactly the kind that needs to be honored and passed on before it disappears.

◆

What I understand now—after years of navigating multicultural environments, after leading conversations across borders and helping organizations avoid the kinds of misunderstandings that once shaped my own journey—is something I could not have put into words as a child sitting across from him at that kitchen table.

My father wasn't just building a career. He was building a mindset.

At the time, I saw sacrifice. I saw movement. I saw long hours and night classes and the quiet determination of a man who refused to stay intimidated by his circumstances. What I didn't see yet was the invisible skill he was developing every single day, in every unfamiliar room he walked into and learned to navigate without a map.

He was learning how to enter spaces where he didn't fully belong—and still find a way to contribute.

He was learning how to listen beyond language.

He was learning how to earn trust across differences.

He was practicing Cultural Intelligence before it had a name in my world.

The same dynamics my father navigated at those Chrysler plants—the cultural friction, the unspoken hierarchies, the daily work of being understood across difference—are the ones I see today in global organizations, just at a different scale and with higher stakes.

People misinterpreting intentions. Leaders assuming their way is the right way. Teams struggling not because of lack of talent, but because of lack of understanding.

The difference is that today, we have language for it. We can name it. We can study it. We can teach it.

But the essence—the lived, daily, quietly heroic practice of crossing cultural distances with curiosity and care—that has been happening for generations, in kitchens and factories and hallways and border towns, long before anyone wrote a book about it.

My father didn't call it CQ when he stayed up late learning English.

He didn't call it CQ when he built relationships that lasted decades across different backgrounds and rose in the ranks of management at an American corporation.

He didn't call it CQ when he chose curiosity over fear in environments that could have easily made him feel small.

But that is exactly what it was.

And that is exactly what lives at the core of my work today.

His story lives inside every framework I build. When I teach leaders to pause before judging behavior, I am thinking about the silent gaps he crossed on his own, without tools, without language, without anyone telling him it had a name. When I ask people to expand their definition of professionalism, I am honoring the man who crossed borders so that his daughter could—and eventually teach others to cross them too.

This work is about awareness. It is about responsibility. And ultimately—it is about choice.

Today, I have the privilege of giving language and structure and strategy to something my father lived instinctively, in the desert light of Torreón and the cooler air of Saltillo and the long fluorescent hallways of a Chrysler plant in Detroit.

I am not teaching something new.

I am translating something I witnessed.

A TOOL TO TAKE WITH YOU

Who was your first CQ mentor—before you had a name for it?

Think of someone in your life who navigated cultural difference with skill and grace, not because they were trained to, but because they paid attention.

A parent. A grandparent. A neighbor. A colleague.

Someone who crossed distances—geographic, cultural, generational—and brought people with them rather than leaving them behind.

Write their name.

Write one specific thing they did—one moment, one habit, one choice—that you are still carrying forward today.

That is your Root.

That is where your cultural intelligence began. Long before you knew what to call it.

Chapter Three

The Girl Who Wanted to Fly

When I was a little girl, I wanted to be a flight attendant.

Our family took a flight to Mexico city as my father received a recognition in a fancy hotel. When I saw those beautiful ladies I was so impressed, one of them talked to me about how she got to travel all over and meet people from all around the world. I just knew that was what I wanted to do. And I know how that sounds, there are more ambitious dreams a girl could have at that age, dreams that arrive already polished and impressive, already pointing toward something the world recognizes as serious. But this one was mine, and it was not small. What I wanted — underneath the uniform— was the world. I wanted to see it. All of it. I wanted to belong to the kind of life where you woke up in a different city and your work required you to move between places where language and flavors were different to my own.

I wanted, in the simplest and most honest terms, to fly.

My father heard this dream and looked at me with the particular expression of a man who loves you enough to want more for you than you have yet thought to want for yourself.

"Think bigger," he said.

So, when the time to choose a career came I thought bigger. And what I arrived at was this: I wanted to be an ambassador.

A woman who represented her country in foreign capitals. Who navigated the space between cultures with authority and grace. Who sat at tables where the decisions about how nations relate to one another are made, and who understood enough of the world to contribute something real to those decisions.

I held this dream quietly for a long time. It felt too large to say out loud. But I carried it—the way you carry something precious that you are not yet sure you have earned the right to want.

Then I was granted a scholarship to ITESM to study International Affairs.

The Tecnológico de Monterrey sits in the foothills of the Sierra Madre Oriental on the northern edge of one of Mexico's largest and most internationally connected cities. It is THE most recognized institution in Latin America. It is the kind of university that takes the ambitions of young people seriously and builds infrastructure around them—the kind that sends its graduates into the world with a particular confidence and a particular set of doors already open. It is also the one that required the highest tuition fee in the country.

From Ramos Arizpe, where we lived, Monterrey was about ninety minutes away. Close enough to be real. Far enough to feel like another world entirely.

I remember the feeling of finding out my high school grades had opened that door. That particular species of joy that comes not just from getting what you want, but from having the world confirm, in writing, that what you wanted was worth having. A scholarship. My name on paper that said: you belong here. You earned this. Come.

I was going to go. The world felt suddenly close enough to touch—not the title, not the foreign capitals, but the first step toward the kind of person who could eventually claim that life.

And then I was told I could not go.

The reason was not academic. It was not financial. It was my father.

He was a reasonable man in most matters. He was, as you have already come to know from the previous chapter, a man of genuine intelligence and quiet courage — someone who had crossed his own borders, built his own bridges, earned trust in rooms where he started as an outsider. He was also a man shaped by his generation, his culture, and a particular kind of love that expresses itself through protection even when protection looks, from the outside, like a wall.

He felt it was unsafe. Not because there was no precedent—there was. There were people in our circle already studying in Monterrey. Either in the university residences or living in a supervised house off campus sharing with other girls watched over by a señora who made sure everyone came home at night and the doors were locked. The structures existed. Other families were already using them. Other fathers had already decided that the world was navigable enough for their daughters.

My father had decided differently. And no amount of evidence to the contrary moved him.

I pushed. I argued. I made the case the way you make cases at that age—with the particular combination of logic and desperation that comes from wanting something so badly you can feel the shape of it in your chest. I told him about the people I knew. I explained the residence, the supervision, the señora. I laid out every reasonable counterargument I could construct.

He listened to all of it.

And then he said something I have never forgotten.

"If you want it so badly," he said, his voice completely calm, "then I will quit my job at Chrysler and find another one in Monterrey. But you are not going alone."

That was the end of it.

I want to pause here and tell you something that took me two decades and a son of my own to understand.

When I tell this story in workshops, people sometimes assume my father was the obstacle. A man who clipped his daughter's wings out of fear or tradition or the particular stubbornness of a generation that did not believe women belonged too far from home. I told it that way myself, for a long time—not consciously, not with cruelty, but with the simplified certainty of someone who had not yet lived enough to see the full picture.

I am a mother now. Mikel is eighteen and heading to college and then, if everything goes as planned, to Paris—and my perspective has shifted. I understand now, in a way I could not have at seventeen, the weight of the decision he made in a moment when no one has all the information everyone is doing their best.

My father said no but also never once complained about the path that no created for him—the adjustments he made, the things he carried quietly so that I could keep going. I did not see that then. I was too busy being the one who had been redirected to notice the one doing the redirecting. Only time and age allow us to see the full picture. He took that hit for me. And he did it with the grace that only unconditional love can provide.

Whatever he could not give me at that moment, he gave me something else: the proof that love sometimes looks like a closed door, and that the farthest school on the map can still be exactly the right one.

◆

He wanted me to study information technology. My mother wanted me to be an architect. Two people who loved me the most, each with a vision of my future that had nothing to do with the one I was trying to build for myself.

And so I did what I have always done when the door I was aiming for closes in front of me.

I found a window.

I took a map of the city of Saltillo and I looked for the school that was farthest from our house. Not the most prestigious. Not the most practical. The farthest. Because if I could not have Monterrey, I was going to have as much distance as the city would give me. I was going to put as much geography as possible between myself and the walls that kept closing around my ambitions.

The school farthest from home was the School of Communication Sciences. That is how I became a communicator.

Not because I had planned it. Not because someone guided me there. Because I looked at a map and chose the farthest point, and the farthest point happened to be the place where I would spend the next years learning how to build bridges between people—how to read an audience, how to craft a message that lands across differences of perspective and expectation and background. How to communicate across distance.

I have thought about that decision many times since. That girl who was not thinking about cultural intelligence. She was not thinking about frameworks or pillars or the book she would one day write about the invisible skill she had been practicing her whole life. She was just sad but determined and looking for the farthest point available.

And the farthest point was exactly the right one.

I want to be careful about how I tell the story of my father's decision. It would be easy to make it simple—a story of a daughter whose ambitions were constrained by a family that did not understand them. That version would be easier to tell. It would also flatten something that was, in reality, much more complicated.

My father loved me with everything he had. The same man who pushed me to think bigger than a flight attendant was the man who could not bring himself to let me go ninety minutes away to study. Both of those things were true at the same time. Both of them were shaped by his culture, his generation, the particular vocabulary that love spoke in the world he had been formed by.

That is what cultural programming looks like from the inside. It does not feel like a cage. It feels like care. And the people inside it are not wrong to love you—they are simply operating from the deepest values available to them, values that were formed long before you arrived and that do not yet have the language to imagine a different way.

Understanding that distinction—between love and limitation, between care and constraint, between the intention behind a cultural value and its actual effect on the person it is applied to—is some of the most important work ROOT asks us to do. Not so we can judge the people who shaped us. But so we can see clearly. So we can name what we were given and what we were redirected away from, and then decide, with full awareness, what we carry forward and what we choose to set down.

A few years later, I was on a plane to France. Not as a flight attendant—as a student, pursuing a master's degree at a university in Grenoble, in a room full of students from twenty-three countries. The ambassador dream did not arrive as a title or a diplomatic posting. It arrived as a life lived across borders—as a career built on the ability to move between cultures with skill and grace, as a framework taught to leaders and organizations who needed exactly that kind of translator.

The dreams did not die. They took the long way.

And today, I am raising Mikel in Mission, Texas—on the border, between two countries, in the particular bilingual, bicultural rhythm of a life that straddles two worlds. He is finishing high school and heading to UTRGV in the fall and Paris in three years. He grew up with a map on his wall and a mother who once pointed him at it blindfolded and said: wherever your finger lands, that is what we learn about this month. He has grown up knowing that the world is navigable—that difference is not a threat but a doorway—because I made sure he knew it.

I made sure because nobody made sure for me.

That is what Root looks like at its fullest. Not just knowing what your culture gave you and what it cost you—but understanding that the story does not end with you. The things you were redirected away from, the scholarship that was not taken, the school on the far side of the map that turned out to be exactly right—they become the ground you build from. They become the reason the next generation walks through doors you never got to open.

◆

The girl who wanted to fly did not become a flight attendant. She did not become an ambassador.

She became something she did not yet have a name for—something that required all of those redirected dreams, all of that accumulated determination, all of the particular texture of a life built across cultures without a map and without permission and with the stubborn, quiet conviction that the world was worth understanding.

She took a city map and found the farthest school. And that was the beginning of everything.

◆

A TOOL TO TAKE WITH YOU

The Three Strengths Inventory.

Write down three specific strengths your culture gave you — not generic strengths, but ones that came directly from your background, your family, the particular life you lived before you had any choice in it.

Resilience counts. So does resourcefulness.

So does the ability to find a window when a door is locked.

Loyalty. Warmth. The instinct to take care of the people around you. The stubbornness that looks like determination from the right angle.

Now write one thing your culture redirected you away from. Not to grieve it. Just to see it clearly.

Because the thing you were redirected away from is often the thing that is still quietly driving you.

That is your Root speaking.

It has been speaking all along.

Chapter Four

Alejandro Walks In

We had made a pact.

There were three of us—Roxana, the one with experience and who opened the door; Gloria, the connector; and me, daring to fly away for the first time. Three Mexican women arriving together for our first week of graduate study at a university in Grenoble, France, in a program that had drawn students from twenty-three countries. We had talked about it on the way there, in the way you talk about things when you are young and nervous and trying to convert your anxiety into intention. Roxana took the lead and made us wake up extra early the first day. We were going to represent Mexico well. We were going to be the Mexicans who arrived on time, dressed professionally, sat in the front row, took careful notes, and made it impossible for anyone in that room to reach for the easy story about who we were before they had actually met us.

Roxana was our anchor. She had already navigated international spaces before France—her ITESM degree had taken her to a Disney internship where she had worked alongside people from a dozen countries, learning in real time what it meant to move between cultures with both competence and warmth. She knew things the rest of us were still figuring out: how to read a room without losing yourself in it, how to be fully present in a place that was not yours without pretending it was. She was the one who set the alarm that first morning. She was the one who led.

She is also, to this day, the one who stayed. Roxana married a French kind man, built a life in that country, and has since traveled to more countries than most people visit in a lifetime. When Mikel and I visited a few years ago, she was our host—generous and unhurried and entirely at home in the world in the way that only people who have genuinely rooted themselves can be. She will be one of the first guests on my podcast, because the cultural intelligence she has lived—quietly, thoroughly, without ever making a performance of it—is exactly the kind of wisdom this work is built to honor.

We knew the story. We had heard it our whole lives—the one that arrives before you do, that travels faster than you can, that waits in the assumptions of people who have never been to your country but feel certain they understand it. That Mexicans are always late. That we are informal, unprofessional, not quite serious. That we are more interested in the party than the work.

We agreed, quietly and collectively, that we were going to be the evidence against that story.

So on the first day of class, we woke up early. We dressed carefully—the kind of careful that is less about vanity than about armor, the deliberate construction of a version of yourself designed to say: look at me before you assume anything. We arrived at the lecture hall with time to spare, chose our seats with intention, arranged our notebooks and our pens, and settled in with the composed alertness of people who are performing competence because they genuinely feel it.

The room filled around us. Students from France, Germany, South Africa, Italy, the United States, China, India, Peru—twenty-three countries finding their seats in the particular shuffle and murmur of a first class, everyone slightly uncertain, everyone performing their own version of readiness.

The professor arrived. The class began.

We had kept our pact perfectly for exactly ten minutes.

Then, a knock came from behind us.

The door at the back of the lecture hall opened, and he walked in. He was Mexican—we knew it immediately, the way you know certain things about your own people before a single word is spoken, something in the posture and the ease and the particular energy of it. His cap was on backwards. He was wearing jeans and a casual shirt. He paused for a moment, scanning the room, getting his bearings with the unhurried confidence of someone who has never felt the need to apologize for being a few minutes late.

And then, in the thickest, most unmistakable Mexico City accent I had ever heard outside of Mexico City, he addressed the professor.

"¿Qué onda, profe? ¿Es aquí la clase?"

What's up, profe. Is this the right class. Every head in that room turned.

And in the two seconds that followed—in the small, suspended silence between his words landing and the class resuming—I felt ten minutes of careful, deliberate, strategic work dissolve as completely as if it had never existed.

I want to describe what that felt like as precisely as I can, because the feeling is important and it is easy to summarize it in a way that loses the texture of it.

It was not anger, exactly. Alejandro had done nothing wrong. He had walked into a classroom. He had greeted a professor. He had been entirely, authentically himself—cheerful, relaxed, unguarded, completely at home in his own skin in a room full of strangers from twenty-three countries on his first day of a graduate program in France. There is something genuinely admirable in that, if you step back far enough to see it clearly.

But I could not step back far enough. Not in that moment.

What I felt was something more complicated than anger—a mixture of helplessness and recognition and a specific kind of exhaustion that comes from understanding, viscerally and immediately, that the work you have been doing is undone. Not because you did it wrong. But because someone else did something that you had no control over, and the room did not distinguish between the two of you. To the twenty-three countries watching from their seats, there was no difference between the women who had arrived early and pressed their clothes and arranged their notebooks—and the man who had strolled in ten minutes late in a backwards cap. We were all, in that moment, Mexicans.

And Mexicans, the story said, were always late.

That is how stereotypes work. Not through malice, usually. Through the economy of the human mind, which looks for patterns and categories and shortcuts because the world has too much information in it to process person by person.

One moment—one entrance, one greeting, one backwards cap—and a category is confirmed for everyone watching. The work you did to complicate that category disappears. The story reasserts itself.

I understood something that morning that I could not have articulated until much later.

I could not control how others saw my culture. I could only control how I showed up within it.

But here is what took me longer to understand—and what I think is actually the deeper truth inside this story.

Alejandro was not wrong to walk in the way he did.

I need to sit with that for a moment, because it is not the comfortable conclusion. The comfortable conclusion is the one I reached first: that Alejandro had been careless, that he had not thought about the stakes, that he had failed some collective responsibility we all had as Mexicans abroad to manage the impression we were making. That conclusion is satisfying in a particular way. It gives me someone to blame for the feeling of helplessness, and it frames the problem as one of individual behavior rather than something larger and harder.

But the more honest conclusion is this: Alejandro was being himself. Completely, uncomplicatedly, authentically himself. He was warm and unguarded and comfortable in his own skin in a foreign country on his first day of graduate school, and those are not small things. His Mexico City accent and his jeans and his easy greeting to the professor were not failures of cultural intelligence. They were expressions of cultural identity—of who he actually was, unperformed and unedited.

The problem was not Alejandro.

The problem was a room full of people who had not yet learned to separate the individual from the category. Who had not yet developed the habit—or been given the tools—to pause before the automatic story arrived and ask: wait. Is what I am seeing actually what I think it is? Or am I reaching for a pattern because patterns are easier than people?

That is the question at the center of the Read pillar. And it is the question I did not yet know how to ask in that lecture hall in Grenoble, because nobody had taught me the framework that would have made it available to me.

I was too busy managing impressions to examine them.

◆

The pact we three women had made that morning was not wrong. It came from somewhere real—from the experience of being underestimated, from the exhaustion of carrying a country's reputation on your back, from the genuine desire to change a story that had been running too long without our input. I do not regret arriving early. I am grateful for Roxana and the pressed clothes and the careful notebook arrangement.

But I have thought about that morning many times since, and what I understand now is that the pact was operating from a position of reaction rather than root.

We were responding to the story others told about us—working backward from their assumptions, trying to preempt their judgment, allowing their framework to determine our behavior before they had said a word.

That is a particular kind of invisible cost. You spend enormous energy managing a narrative that was never yours to begin with. You adapt—not to build a bridge, but to avoid a judgment. And the exhaustion of that kind of adaptation is cumulative and quiet and very hard to name while you are inside it.

Root asks you to do something different. It asks you to understand your culture so clearly—its strengths, its defaults, its inherited wisdom and its inherited limitations—that you can bring it into any room from a position of knowledge rather than defense. Not performing it. Not apologizing for it. Not managing it. Simply knowing it, and choosing, deliberately, how to carry it forward.

The woman who does that does not need Alejandro not to walk in. She does not need the room to be different. She is grounded enough in who she is that the room's assumptions do not determine her. They inform her. And from that clarity, she can decide how to respond—not react, respond—with intention and with the full weight of everything she actually is.

That woman was not me, that morning in Grenoble. But she is who I was working toward.

Alejandro finished the program. He traveled everywhere, lived fully, and moved through the world with the same charm and warmth that has taken him everywhere since—most recently to Italy, where he has built yet another chapter of a life that seems to accumulate adventures the way other people accumulate responsibilities.

He is my friend. Genuinely, lastingly, in the way that people from a shared foreign experience sometimes become friends for life. About twelve years ago, his father died. He did not call first. He just drove—fourteen hours straight—and arrived at my house in the middle of his grief, needing somewhere safe to land.

He stayed a few days. He was good with Mikel in the way that warm, present people often are with children—easy and unguarded and not performing anything. He became my son's compadre before either of them quite knew what that meant.

He says he will visit Mikel in Paris when the time comes and take him out for a drink.

I sincerely hope he is joking. I am fairly certain he is not.

What I know is that he taught me something that morning in Grenoble without knowing he was teaching me anything at all.

He taught me that culture is not a costume you put on for difficult rooms. It is not a performance you calibrate for an audience. It walks in with you whether you have thought about it or not—in your accent, in your posture, in the way you greet a professor on your first day in a foreign country. It is always already there.

The question Root asks is not whether your culture will be present. It will be. It always is.

The question is whether you will be present with it—aware of what you are carrying, clear about what it means, and grounded enough to bring it forward as something chosen rather than something that simply happens to you while you are busy trying to fit in.

Ten minutes of a pact could not protect me from that room.

But twenty years of Root eventually gave me something better than protection. It gave me a place to stand.

A TOOL TO TAKE WITH YOU

The Cultural Audit.

Your culture walks into every room with you—whether you know it or not. This exercise is about making it visible.

Write one sentence for each of the following: What does my culture say about time?

(Is punctuality respect? Is flexibility warmth? Is early arrival eagerness or anxiety?)

What does my culture say about authority?

(Do you challenge it openly? Defer to it quietly? Navigate around it?)

What does my culture say about how disagreement should sound? (Direct and immediate? Indirect and diplomatic? Avoided entirely?)

What does my culture say about who speaks first in a room?

Now ask: in which of these has your culture served you?

And in which of these has it created friction you did not fully understand until after the fact?

You do not need to change your answers. You just need to see them.

That seeing is Root.

Chapter Five

The Blindfold and the Map

There is a map on the wall of my memory that I return to more often than almost any other image from Mikel's childhood.

It is a world map—the kind with the countries in different colors and the oceans in pale blue and all the names of places printed in small, serious type that makes the world look simultaneously enormous and knowable. We hung it where he could reach it. That was the point.

Once a month, on a Sunday, he would stand in front of it with a blindfold on. He would spin slowly, reach out, and press his finger to wherever it landed. Then he would pull the blindfold off and look at where he was pointing.

That country—whatever it was, wherever his finger had found it—was ours for the next few hours. Sometimes for the week.

He was somewhere between six and eight when we started. Old enough to find it exciting. Young enough that the world was still entirely a place of wonder rather than a place of logistics.

◆

The exercise had one rule. Just one.

He was allowed to say he didn't like it but he was not allowed to refuse to try.

The distinction matters more than it might seem. I was not trying to manufacture enthusiasm. I was not trying to convince him that everything was equally wonderful or that his preferences didn't exist. Children are people—they have genuine reactions to things, and pretending otherwise teaches them to mistrust their own instincts. What I wanted was something different and more durable: the habit of encountering something unfamiliar and choosing curiosity over refusal. The knowledge, built slowly across many Sundays, that the unfamiliar is navigable. That it will not hurt you to try.

Once the country was chosen, Mikel chose three things he wanted to explore. The options were open: food, language, music, clothing, history, geography, traditions, stories. He could pick anything, in any combination. I would write them down.

Then we figured out how to get there from Mission, Texas.

I should tell you how the blindfold map came to exist, because the origin of it matters.

I had decided that Sundays would be unplugged. No devices—no screens, no phones, no tablets, no background television. I wanted one day a month that belonged to something other than the digital current that was pulling us both in opposite directions. Without any family close by, no cousins to play with on Saturdays or breakfast with grandparents after church on Sunday, I thought this was a reasonable and even generous idea. I presented it to Mikel with the quiet confidence of a parent who believes she has made a decision.

He looked at me for a moment.

"Okay," he said. "But you have to do it too." He was six years old.

I agreed—because he was right, and because I had not quite anticipated that he would call my bluff so immediately and so completely. If the day was going to be unplugged, it was going to be unplugged for both of us. There would be no quiet checking of emails while he was occupied with something analog. There would be no exception for work, even for just a minute, or if something important that had come up.

The map was my solution to the question of what we would actually do with ourselves on those Sundays without our devices. It turned out to be one of the best things I have ever stumbled into.

The Sundays blur together now into a single warm impression—the two of us at the kitchen table, or at the library, or in the car heading toward a restaurant we had never tried, or standing in an aisle of an international grocery store reading the labels on things we couldn't pronounce. But there are specific memories that rise above the blur and stay.

The day his finger landed somewhere in the Middle East.

He chose food, as he often did. And language. We drove to a Lebanese restaurant in the Valley and he tried falafel for the first time—sitting across from me with the focused attention of a child who has agreed to take the exercise seriously, picking it up, examining it, putting it in his mouth. Chewing. Thinking. The particular expression of someone genuinely evaluating something new rather than performing an opinion.

He liked it. Not immediately, not without reservation, but genuinely—the kind of like that surprises you.

And then we learned our greeting. We practiced it on the drive home, saying it back and forth until it felt less foreign in our mouths.

Wasalam alekum.

Peace be upon you.

He said it to me again that evening when I told him it was time for bed. With a perfectly straight face.

I cannot describe how much I loved that child in that moment.

What I did not fully understand at the time—though I think I felt it—was that those Sunday mornings were not just entertainment. They were not an elaborate way to keep a six-year-old away from a screen.

They were cultural intelligence practice. Monthly. Embodied. Low-stakes enough to be enjoyable, and real enough to actually work.

Every time Mikel stood in front of that map with his blindfold on, he was practicing the foundational skill of Root: the willingness to encounter difference before it is required of you. Not in a crisis, not in a professional setting where something is on the line, not in a moment where you have to perform competence under pressure—but on a Sunday morning, in your own house, with your mother, with a plate of falafel and a greeting you are still getting your mouth around.

The world is enormous and it is not evenly distributed in the rooms we happen to grow up in. Most of us reach adulthood having had deep contact with our own culture and shallow or accidental contact with most others. We arrive at our first international meeting or our first diverse workplace or our first relationship across a significant cultural difference having never once practiced the muscle that moment requires. And we wonder why it feels so difficult.

Mikel was practicing that muscle at six. Because every Sunday, something landed under his finger that was not Mission, Texas. And every Sunday, he chose three things to understand about it.

He is eighteen now. He eats almost everything. He is curious about people in the particular way that comes not from having been told to be curious, but from having had curiosity built into the rhythm of his childhood until it became simply who he is. He is heading to UTRGV in the fall, and then—if everything goes as planned—to Paris, to Le Cordon Bleu, to learn the craft he has chosen with the same focused attention he brought to a plate of falafel on a Sunday afternoon in the Rio Grande Valley.

I cannot take credit for who he is. Children build themselves, largely, from materials we don't fully control. But I can say that I tried to make sure one of those materials was a world map on the wall and a blindfold and one Sunday a month where we put our phones down and went somewhere together without leaving the house.

Root is often taught as a practice of looking inward—of understanding your own culture before you try to navigate anyone else's. And that is true. It is where we have spent the last several chapters, turning the lens on ourselves, examining what we were given before we had any choice in the matter.

But Root has an outward dimension too. It is not only about knowing what you carry. It is about building the habit of encountering difference before you need to — so that when you are sitting in a conference room in Indiana or a lecture hall in Grenoble or a negotiation in Monterrey, you have already done this before. The unfamiliar does not throw you, because you have been practicing the unfamiliar your whole life. You have eaten the falafel. You know the greeting. You have stood in front of the map enough times that the enormous world feels, if not familiar, then at least navigable.

That is what I was trying to give Mikel. Not a curriculum. Not a lesson plan. Just the repeated, embodied, pleasurable experience of encountering something he didn't know and finding that it was worth knowing.

The practice is available to all of us. It does not require a world map or a blindfold or a child who will hold you accountable to your own rules. It requires only the decision to go somewhere new before you are required to, to try something unfamiliar before the stakes are high, to learn a greeting in a language that is not yours for no reason other than the simple and radical act of saying: this place and its people are worth the effort of my attention.

Wasalam alekum. Peace be upon you.

Start there, if you need somewhere to start.

The Sundays were not always easy. Staying away from devices was harder than I expected—for both of us, but especially for me. There were mornings when the pull of the phone felt almost physical, when I was aware of emails accumulating and messages waiting and the particular low-grade anxiety of being unreachable. There were Sundays when Mikel was tired or resistant, when the exercise felt like work rather than play, when I wondered if I was simply imposing my own cultural preoccupations on a child who would have been perfectly happy watching a movie.

But we kept going. And somewhere in the keeping-going, the Sundays started giving us things we had not planned for.

One year, the map—or perhaps just good timing—led us to China in the middle of Lunar New Year. The IMAS museum in McAllen was celebrating, and we went. I remember walking in to the sound of drums and the particular energy of a crowd that is genuinely festive rather than performing festivity. The dragons were moving through the space—long, luminous, carried by a dozen people working together in perfect coordination, weaving between visitors who stepped aside with a kind of instinctive delight. There was food, and music, and color everywhere, and Mikel stood in the middle of it with his eyes wide and his phone — because by that age the rule had evolved—firmly in his pocket.

He turned to me at one point and said: "This is real, right? Like this is actually what they do?"

Yes, I told him. This is actually what they do.

He nodded slowly, the way he does when he is filing something away permanently.

I think about that afternoon when people ask me how you raise a child with cultural intelligence in a border town in South Texas, far from the international schools and global cities where that kind of upbringing is assumed to be available. The answer is: you go to the museum when the dragons are there. You eat the falafel. You say the greeting on the drive home. You put the phone down and you show up—fully, actually, with your whole attention—to whatever piece of the world has landed under your finger that Sunday.

It does not require a passport. It requires presence. That is all Root ever asks of you.

I showed him the world before the world required anything of him.

I hope, when he is standing in a kitchen in Paris or a boardroom somewhere neither of us can currently imagine, that some Sunday morning in Mission, Texas comes back to him. Not as a lesson. Just as a feeling. The feeling of putting your hand on a map and trusting that wherever it lands, there is something worth understanding.

That is Root. Practiced in the smallest possible way. On a Sunday morning. With a blindfold. With a boy who made sure his mother put her phone down too.

A TOOL TO TAKE WITH YOU

The Weekly Cultural Moment.

You do not need a world map or a child or a Sunday ritual.

You need one small, regular encounter with something unfamiliar.

Choose one thing this week: Cook one dish from a culture you have never cooked from before. Learn one greeting in a language you do not speak.

Find a cultural event in your city you have never attended—a festival, a museum exhibition, a community celebration—and go.

Read one article, watch one documentary, or find one book about a place your finger would land if you closed your eyes and pointed at a map.

The rule is the same rule I gave Mikel: You are allowed to decide you don't love it. You are not allowed to decide before you try.

Do this once a week for a month.

Notice what changes in how you move through the world.

That is Root, practiced forward.

That is what it looks like when cultural intelligence becomes not a skill you apply—but a person you are.

✦

READ

"Most people do not listen with the intent to understand. They listen with the intent to reply."
— *Stephen R. Covey*

Chapter Six

The Name on the Screen

It was summer. The kind of summer that Indiana does well—thick with heat even in air-conditioned rooms, the sky outside the conference center windows a flat, pale blue that looked nothing like home.

I was in my late twenties. I had flown in from Reynosa for a major supplier conference, the kind that gathers executives from companies with names you recognize from the side of buildings. The room was large and formal, set up in the style of corporate events the world over: rows of chairs angled toward a stage, the low hum of projectors warming up, coffee stations along the back wall that nobody was paying attention to yet.

I found my seat and settled in. Around me, the room filled with executives—mostly men, mostly Asian, some American. Suits. Name badges. The particular energy of people who are used to being important in their industries and know it. I smoothed my jacket, checked my badge, and told myself I belonged there. I had worked for this. I had earned this seat.

I almost believed it.

◆

My boss—a Japanese American man, brilliant and precise—stood at the front of the room and began introducing our team. One by one, our names appeared on the screen behind him. Photographs beside each name. Titles. Roles. A full organizational chart of doers.

I watched from the audience as my colleagues were called, each acknowledgment brief and professional, a quick ripple of attention moving through the room before settling again. And then I saw my own name appear on the screen.

Large. Projected. Impossible to miss.

Every head in that room turned toward me.

And in the space of those two or three seconds—that tiny, enormous window between my name appearing and the room's attention moving on—I felt something I had not expected to feel. Not pride. Not confidence. Something quieter and harder to name. A sudden, acute awareness of being the only one. The only woman. The only Mexican. The only face in that room that looked like mine.

I wanted to say something. Not just to acknowledge the moment, but to plant a flag—to let that room know exactly who was in it. I wanted to say

Buenos días.

Two words. My words. The greeting I had spoken every morning of my professional life, the one that lived in my chest like something inherited, like something true.

I said nothing.

I smiled. I nodded. I let the moment pass the way I had learned to let things pass — quietly, efficiently, without disruption. Years of practice had made it almost effortless, that particular movement of swallowing something real and replacing it with something acceptable.

The conference continued. My boss finished his introductions. The first presenter took the stage. And I sat in my chair in Indiana with the strange, hollow aftertaste of a moment I had chosen not to claim.

I told myself it was the right call. Professional. Appropriate. Savvy, even—the kind of reading-the-room that gets you ahead in global business. And maybe it was. But there was something underneath that rationalization that I couldn't quite shake loose, something that would take me years to properly name.

I had not stayed silent because the room was wrong for Buenos días.

I had stayed silent because somewhere along the way, I had decided that I was wrong for it.

That is a different thing entirely.

A few years later, I was working for Motorola, and everything changed with a door.

It was my first morning visiting the New York office—a tall, glass-and-steel building that hummed with the particular energy of American corporate life, all efficient movement and purposeful noise. My new boss met me in the lobby. He was warm, easy, the kind of person who makes you feel immediately at ease in an unfamiliar city. He gave me a tour—the open floor plan, the conference rooms with their whiteboards already covered in diagrams, the kitchen where someone had brought in bagels for a Tuesday for no apparent reason.

"And more importantly," he said, with a small smile, "let me show you where the cafeteria is."

We laughed. We walked. The hallway was long and bright, afternoon light coming through the windows on the left side, the kind of light that makes everything look slightly more promising than it is.

And then we reached a glass door.

He got there first. Without hesitation—without even thinking about it, I could tell—he reached out, pulled it open, and held it. Waiting. For me to walk through first.

I stepped through the door.

And something cracked open in my chest.

It took me a moment to understand what I was feeling. Not gratitude, exactly—though that was part of it. Something more disorienting than gratitude.

Something that arrived with the particular weight of recognition. I had not walked through a door first in years.

Not because my Japanese colleagues were unkind. They were not. But in Japanese professional culture, hierarchy moves through space as naturally as it moves through language. Seniority leads. Juniors follow. Women, especially in the corporate environments I had worked in, often walked behind. It was not a statement. It was simply the order of things, so deeply embedded in the rhythm of daily life that I had stopped noticing it.

I had adapted to it so completely that I had forgotten it wasn't the only way.

Standing in that hallway in New York, with one unremarkable act of courtesy from a man who was simply doing what his culture had taught him to do, I understood something I had been carrying without knowing it. I had spent years learning to navigate spaces that were not made for me. And in that navigation, in that constant, invisible work of adjustment and accommodation, I had left pieces of myself in corridors I could no longer find my way back to.

When did I stop walking first? When did I stop saying Buenos días?

I want to be careful here, because this story is not a simple one and I do not want to flatten it into something it is not.

I have spent more than twenty years working alongside Japanese colleagues and inside Japanese corporate culture. I have genuine respect—deep respect—for what that culture holds. The precision. The commitment. The way relationships are built slowly and honored completely. I have been shaped by those years in ways I am still discovering.

Adaptation is not the enemy. Adaptation is, in many ways, the whole point of cultural intelligence. You cannot connect across cultures without it.

But there is a difference between choosing to adapt and forgetting that you ever had a choice.

The Indiana conference room and the Motorola hallway were not dramatic moments. Nobody was cruel. Nothing was deliberately taken from me. And yet in both of them, quietly, the same thing was happening: I was disappearing into the expectations of my environment, one small adjustment at a time, until the woman I had been before all those adjustments felt like someone I used to know.

That is the cost that doesn't show up on a performance review. That is the cost nobody warns you about.

◆

I work for a Japanese company again now. And I adapt, still—because adaptation is a skill I have earned and I use it deliberately. But I also walk through doors first when I get there first. I say Buenos días in the morning when it is what I feel. I carry my culture into the rooms I enter the way I carry my name: not as an apology, and not as a performance, but simply as what is true about me.

The Cultural Lens™ did not teach me to stop adapting. It taught me to notice when I was doing it—and to ask myself, honestly, whether I had chosen it or whether it had simply happened to me while I was busy trying to fit in.

That noticing is everything.

It is, in fact, where Read begins.

✦

A TOOL TO TAKE WITH YOU

The Room Audit.

Think of the three rooms you walk into most regularly—at work, at home, in your community.

Whose cultural lens are you using to navigate each one?

And whose lens is actually driving the decisions being made there?

Now ask yourself: in which of those rooms have you stopped walking first? What did you leave at the door to get through it?

And do you remember making that choice—or did it just happen?

Write it down. That list is the beginning of your Read.

Chapter Seven

What Feels Like Exclusion Might Be Respect

There is a version of this story I could tell that would make me the victim of it.

I have told that version, privately, to myself—in the moment when it was happening, in the hours after, in the particular way that the mind rehearses its grievances when it is trying to make sense of something that felt wrong. In that version, I was sidelined. Dismissed. Made invisible by a system that did not value what I brought to the room. In that version, the instruction I received was a small injustice—quiet, professional, the kind that leaves no marks but costs something anyway.

That version of the story is understandable. And it is incomplete.

The fuller version—the one I arrived at after twenty years of working in multicultural environments, after enough experience to slow down my first reaction and ask a second question—is more interesting. And more useful.

It is the version this chapter is about.

But I did not arrive at it quickly. I arrived at it the way you arrive at most things worth understanding: slowly, imperfectly, through a series of moments that confused me before they taught me.

Let me show you three of them.

The first lesson came from a corner.

I was doing a walk-through of our warehouse floor with one of our Japanese coordinators—a professional, courteous man who had been with the company for years and who navigated the environment with the quiet precision of someone who had internalized its rules so completely that following them no longer felt like effort. We were talking as we walked, easy conversation, the kind that happens when two people who work well together are simply moving through a shared space.

And then we came to a corner.

There was nothing in the middle. No obstruction, no equipment, no safety line to respect. The diagonal path was shorter. It made obvious, practical sense to cut across. So I did.

He did not say anything. But I felt his reaction before I saw it—the particular quality of attention that shifts when someone near you has done something they consider significant. I turned, and he was looking at me with an expression I could not immediately read. Not anger. Not contempt. Something closer to the look you give a child who has just demonstrated, without knowing it, that they have not yet learned something important.

We continued the walk-through. On the way back, I cut the corner again. And this time he spoke.

"Why do you do that?" he asked. Politely. Genuinely curious.

I explained the obvious: it was shorter. There was nothing in the way. It saved a few steps.

He considered this. And then he said something that I have carried with me ever since.

"Following the rules has a purpose," he said. "If we cut one corner, it becomes easier to cut the next. And then the next. And what looks like a small thing here becomes a habit that costs us somewhere we cannot see yet."

He was not talking about the warehouse floor.

He was talking about a philosophy of organizational discipline that runs so deep in Japanese corporate culture that it expresses itself in the way a person walks around a corner. Not as a performance of compliance. As a genuine belief that consistency in small things is what makes reliability in large ones possible. That the invisible habits shape the visible outcomes.

I had cut a corner. He had seen a worldview.

That is Read. And I had not yet learned how to do it.

◆

The second lesson came from a training room—and from a colleague who was trying, very sincerely, to understand something that made no sense to him.

A trainer had flown in from the Midwest to facilitate a leadership session for our team. It was a good program—thoughtful, well-resourced, with practical tools for building a more positive work environment. We moved through the material together until we reached an exercise. The trainer divided us into small groups and gave each group a scenario to discuss and present back to the class.

Our scenario involved unions—specifically, the fundamental difference between how labor conflict is managed in Japan versus North America.

My colleague was struggling. He was an intelligent man, a hard worker, someone who genuinely wanted to understand what he was being shown. But the more the trainer explained, the more frustrated he became. He kept returning to the same point: if Japanese corporate culture is so cooperative, if everything is oriented toward harmony and mutual benefit, why would a union even be necessary? What was there to resolve, if everyone was already working together?

He was not being dismissive. He was being genuinely confused by something that, from inside his cultural framework, did not add up. He said, with real frustration: "It seems like everything in Japan is just pink and bubbles. Everybody helps each other. So why do they need a union? It doesn't make sense."

The trainer offered examples. Drew parallels. Tried several angles. And my colleague kept arriving at the same wall—not because he was unwilling, but because the lens he was looking through could not resolve the image.

I raised my hand.

"If I may," I said, "I think the difference is cultural. And the key is one word."

I said: when we think about Japan, you have to start with the collective. Everything—from how decisions are made to how conflict is framed to what a successful resolution looks like—is organized around what is good for the group. Not the individual. Not the manager. Not even the company, exactly, but the collective whole of which the company is a part.

When you apply that lens to a union dispute, the goal shifts entirely. A resolution is not a win for one side. It is a finding that the collective can live with—something that honors the relationship between the organization and its people rather than drawing a line between them.

Then I said: now think about North America, and think about culture of individual. Because that is the organizing principle here. The individual's rights. The individual's compensation. The individual's protection from the organization. That is not a flaw—it is a reflection of deeply held cultural values about autonomy and self-determination. But it produces a completely different kind of union, with a completely different approach to conflict, because the fundamental question being asked is different.

In Japan: what outcome can we reach together?

In North America: what am I entitled to?

Both are coherent within their own framework. Both are the product of generations of cultural values expressing themselves through institutional design. Neither is wrong. They are simply answering different questions—because the cultures that produced them were asking different ones.

Japan is a culture of the collective. America of the individual.

Everyone stood quiet for a moment. And then something shifted in his expression—the particular look of a person who has just found the organizing principle that makes a confusing thing legible. "Now, that actually makes sense."

That is Read being used as a bridge. Not to impose one framework on another, but to give someone the lens that allows them to see what they could not see before. The trainer had the content. I had the cultural context. Between us, we got a simple concept to a place of understanding that neither of us could have reached alone.

The third lesson came from a ship.

Not a literal one. But the image my boss gave me one afternoon changed how I understood everything about presenting information to senior leadership in a Japanese corporate environment—and about the profound difference between how cultures think about time, decision-making, and the weight of a single choice.

Our team had been struggling. We were deeply operational in our thinking—comfortable with the daily rhythms of procurement and supply chain management, fluent in the language of execution—but we kept failing when we tried to present our work at the executive level. We would prepare. We would organize. We would try to elevate our thinking from operational to strategic. And we would walk out of those presentations knowing we had not landed the way we needed to.

My boss sat with us after one such session and offered a reframe that I have used every time I have prepared to present to Japanese leadership since.

"Think about a massive ship," he said. "One of those enormous ocean vessels. When that ship is underway, changing its course is not a simple matter. It requires time, planning, and the full awareness that even a minor deviation from the current heading—executed right now—will translate into a significant displacement from the original destination by the time you arrive. The further along the journey, the more consequential the adjustment."

He paused. Then: "That is how Japanese executives think about decisions."

Every proposal presented to that leadership team was being evaluated not only for what it suggested right now, but for where it would take the organization in five years, ten years, twenty years—and how reversible it was if the direction turned out to be wrong. Decisions are not made lightly not because the executives are slow, but because they understand that in an organization of that scale, a course correction is enormously costly. The discipline is in the upfront analysis. The rigor is in the preparation. The value is in the certainty that what you are proposing has been thought through completely before a single degree of heading has been changed.

Once I understood that, everything about how to present to those executives became clear.

They did not want to be surprised. They did not want to discover a risk they had not been told about. They were not looking for creativity in the room—they were looking for evidence that the person presenting had done the work of anticipating consequences before arriving. That the proposal was not an idea but a studied recommendation. That the speaker understood the weight of what they were asking.

We stopped presenting operational updates dressed as strategy. We started presenting scenarios, risk analyses, long-term implications. We studied our audience before we built our slides. We asked not "what do we want to tell them" but "what do they need to see from us to feel confident that we have thought this through."

Our presentations changed. Our credibility changed with them.

And the lesson was not about presentations. It was about the deepest possible expression of Read: not just observing what a culture does differently, but understanding why—tracing the behavior back to the value system that produces it, and then letting that understanding shape how you show up.

The three stories above were preparation for the moment I want to tell you about now.

We were preparing for an audit.

In the manufacturing environment I worked in, audits are significant events—they arrive with preparation checklists and briefing documents and a particular heightening of attention across the plant floor. This one involved a senior auditor visiting from Japan. His English was limited. His expertise was not. He was arriving to evaluate our processes, our documentation, our compliance—the kind of thorough, methodical review that Japanese corporate culture approaches with a precision that I had come to deeply respect over years of working alongside it.

Our local head auditor—who flew in from corporate headquarters in Michigan and knew Japanese business culture well—gathered us in advance to walk through preparation. She was organized and clear, moving through her checklist with the efficiency of someone who had done this many times and understood exactly what was required.

And then she came to me.

"When the auditor arrives," she said, "I'd recommend that you not speak to him directly."

She said it matter-of-factly, the way you deliver information you consider practical rather than personal. She explained: in Japanese business culture, it is customary for a manager to represent their team in formal situations. For a subordinate to speak directly to a visiting senior figure—bypassing the established hierarchy—would reflect poorly on my boss. It would signal a lack of organizational structure. It would, in the particular language of Japanese professional culture, be read as a form of disrespect.

She was not telling me to be invisible. She was telling me how visibility works in a different cultural system.

I understood this intellectually, in the moment she said it. What I felt was something else entirely.

◆

I want to be precise about the feeling, because the feeling is the most important part of this chapter.

It was not rage. It was not the sharp, clarifying anger of someone who has been clearly wronged. It was something quieter and more disorienting—the particular sensation of being told, by someone who meant well, to step back from a room you had worked to earn your place in.

The instruction was professional. It was culturally informed. It was, by every measure of Japanese business practice, correct. And it still landed in my chest with the particular weight of all the other times I had been asked, in one way or another, to make myself smaller for the comfort of a system I had not designed.

I thought about David. Four words on an evaluation form. I thought about Indiana, the conference room, the name on the screen, the choice not to say Buenos días.

And I thought: here we are again.

The difference this time was that I had enough experience to pause before that thought settled into something permanent. To hold it gently. To ask the question that twenty years of navigating multicultural environments had slowly, imperfectly, taught me to ask.

Whose cultural framework am I using to interpret what just happened?

Because I already knew the answer. I had learned it walking around a warehouse corner. I had learned it in the training room when I explained collective versus individual to a frustrated colleague. I had learned it when I finally understood the ocean vessel—that decisions in this culture carry a weight that requires a particular quality of preparation and a particular quality of deference.

The manager who speaks for their team in a formal audit is not diminishing the team. They are honoring it. The subordinate who stays quiet is not invisible. They are demonstrating discipline and trust in the system that holds them. Silence, in that context, is not absence. It is a form of presence—the particular presence of someone who understands their role and fulfills it with integrity.

What feels like exclusion in one culture is a form of respect in another.

I followed the guidance. When the auditor arrived, I observed rather than engaged directly. I watched my boss represent our team with the precision the situation required. I supported from behind the established structure, the way a strong foundation supports a building without being visible from the street.

The audit went well.

And in the observing—in the particular attention that becomes available when you are not focused on contributing your own voice—I noticed things I might have missed otherwise. How the auditor moved through a room. Where he paused and where he did not. The quality of attention he brought to documentation versus process. The moments where his body language settled and the moments where it sharpened.

I was reading him, through his lens rather than mine. And what I read was a man doing serious, careful work in an environment that had been structured to make him feel respected. The structure was working. The audit was working. And I was learning something no direct conversation could have taught me, because I had been quiet enough to watch.

I think about these three stories often when I work with leaders who are managing multicultural teams—particularly leaders who come from cultures where directness is a virtue, where speaking up is how you demonstrate engagement, where silence is associated with disinterest or disrespect.

Those leaders are not wrong. In their cultural framework, they are reading the room accurately. The problem is that they are reading it through the only lens they have been given—and a room full of people from different cultural backgrounds does not operate by a single set of rules.

The team member who does not speak in the meeting is not disengaged. They may be from a culture where you think before you speak, where public disagreement with a superior is a form of disrespect, where the appropriate time to raise a concern is in private rather than in the group.

The colleague who agrees with everything in the room and then quietly does something different is not being deceptive. They may be from a culture where direct refusal is considered impolite, where harmony in the moment is valued over conflict, where the agreement you gave in public is understood by everyone as provisional.

The supplier who takes three meetings before committing to anything is not stalling. They are building the relationship that, in their cultural framework, must exist before a business agreement can be trusted.

The executive who needs a fully developed risk analysis before moving on a proposal is not being slow or bureaucratic. They are captaining a vessel that cannot easily change course—and they need to know that the person presenting has understood the weight of what they are asking.

None of these behaviors are failures. They are signals. And Read is the practice of learning to receive them—accurately, without the distortion of your own cultural defaults—so that you can respond in a way that actually reaches the person you are trying to reach.

What feels like exclusion might be respect.

What feels like evasion might be relationship-building.

What feels like silence might be the most attentive listening in the room.

What feels like obstruction might be the discipline of a culture that takes decisions seriously.

The question is not which interpretation is correct. The question is whether you have done the work to have more than one interpretation available.

I have spent twenty years learning Japanese business culture—not in a classroom, but in the particular way you learn things when they are the daily environment of your professional life. I have made mistakes in that learning. I have misread signals, misjudged moments, walked across corners that I did not yet know carried meaning.

But I have also come to hold a genuine appreciation for what that culture taught me about Read. About the layers of meaning that exist beneath the surface of any professional interaction. About the way respect travels—not always in the directions you were raised to expect, not always in the register you recognize as warmth, but present nonetheless, doing its work, waiting for someone with the patience and the framework to receive it.

The day I was told not to speak directly to the auditor, I felt something I might once have called exclusion.

What I actually received, if I am willing to read it clearly, was an invitation into a different understanding of what it means to be part of a team.

That is what Read offers you. Not the erasure of your first reaction. Not the pretense that cultural difference is always comfortable or always easy to navigate. But the honest, practiced, difficult willingness to stay in the room with your discomfort long enough to ask: what else might be true here?

The answer, when you are willing to look for it, is almost always more interesting than the story you started with.

◆

A TOOL TO TAKE WITH YOU

The Before-You-React Pause.

The next time a cross-cultural interaction triggers a negative feeling — a sense of being dismissed, disrespected, ignored, or excluded — pause before you respond. Not forever. Just long enough to ask three questions in order: One: What did I actually observe?

(Not what I interpreted. What literally happened.)

Two: What cultural value might explain this behavior in the other person's framework—not mine?

(Hierarchy? Collective versus individual? Risk discipline?

A different definition of respect? The weight of a decision that cannot easily be reversed?)

Three: Is my reaction based on what actually happened — or on what I expected to happen, based on my own cultural defaults?

You do not need to abandon your first reaction.

You just need to make room for a second one.

That room is where Read lives.

The more you practice this pause, the faster it becomes.

And the faster it becomes, the more of the room you actually see.

Chapter Eight

The other side of the desk—David's Chapter

A note before we begin.

I do not know what David was thinking. I want to be honest about that from the first sentence, because this chapter is going to do something unusual—it is going to try to see through his eyes, to inhabit his perspective, to follow the logic of his decisions from the inside. And I cannot do that with certainty. I was not in his head. I am working from imagination informed by experience—from twenty years of working alongside people like David, of learning how American corporate culture thinks about professionalism and boundaries and what constitutes appropriate workplace behavior.

What follows is my best attempt to see him clearly. Not to excuse him. Not to condemn him. But to understand the lens he was looking through—because understanding that lens is the only way to interrupt the pattern it created.

The names in this chapter, as throughout this book, have been changed to protect the people whose stories intersect with mine. The evaluation was real. The four words were real. The year without a salary increase was real.

And the lesson—the one that took me years to find—is the most important one in this book.

◆

David had flown in from Indiana.

He was organized—the kind of organized that expresses itself in color-coded folders and printed agendas and the particular satisfaction of a well-structured day. He had prepared for this trip carefully. He had his evaluation forms. He had his notes from the year, accumulated in a spreadsheet he maintained with the same methodical attention he brought to everything he managed. He took his responsibilities seriously. This was not a man who showed up unprepared.

He managed her remotely, from a corporate office thousands of miles away, while she worked daily on the factory floor in Reynosa. Different cities. Different rhythms. Different worlds. The distance required a kind of trust he had learned to calibrate carefully—check-ins, reports, the occasional visit to put a face to the work he was overseeing from Indiana.

He believed in fairness. He believed in consistency. He believed—genuinely, without irony—that the standards he applied to professional behavior should be applied equally to everyone, regardless of where they worked or what background they came from. Equal standards, he had been taught, was what respect looked like.

He was about to learn that equal standards and equitable understanding are not the same thing.

◆

The thing that bothered him had been building for months.

It was not dramatic. It was not a single incident he could point to and say: there, that was the moment. It was more like a low-grade discomfort that accumulated across visits and calls and secondhand reports—something that did not fit the professional framework he had been trained in and that he did not have the language to name precisely.

It was the greetings.

Every time he visited the plant, there she was—his direct report, competent and hardworking and clearly well-regarded by everyone around her—greeting people with a kiss. Not a handshake. Not a professional nod. A kiss. On the cheek. Men and women alike. Colleagues, suppliers, visitors. It happened constantly, automatically, as naturally as breathing.

In the world David had grown up in—in the American Midwest, in the corporate culture he had been formed by, in the HR trainings he had attended about appropriate workplace conduct—physical contact between colleagues was a carefully regulated thing. You shook hands. You kept a professional distance. You did not touch people's faces. These were not arbitrary rules. They were, in his understanding, the architecture of a respectful workplace—a system designed to protect everyone, to ensure that no one felt uncomfortable, to create an environment where people could focus on the work without the complexity of physical contact blurring the professional lines.

He watched her kiss a supplier on the cheek during a site visit. He watched her kiss a colleague she passed in the corridor.

He watched, and he felt the low-grade discomfort become something more specific. Something he felt a responsibility to address.

He wrote it down.

He did not write it down with malice. I want to be precise about that, because malice would be simpler—simpler to feel, simpler to condemn, simpler to move past. What David felt was something closer to professional responsibility. He had a duty of care to the people he managed and to the environment he oversaw. He had observed behavior that, by the standards he had been trained in, was inappropriate. He documented it. He brought it to HR. He addressed it directly in the evaluation.

He thought he was doing his job. He thought he was being fair and consistent.

He thought—and this is the part that matters most—that the standard he was applying was neutral. Universal. Simply the correct way that professional environments should function, regardless of where they were located or who was in them.

He did not know that neutrality is a fiction. That every professional standard is cultural—shaped by the particular history and values of the environment that produced it. That what feels like an objective rule is almost always someone's default, elevated to the status of universal truth because that someone had enough power to make it stick.

He did not know that the woman sitting across from him was operating from a completely different and equally valid framework. That in her world—in Reynosa, in Mexico, across much of Latin America—a kiss on the cheek was not a boundary violation. It was the boundary. The physical, warm, human acknowledgment that said: I see you as a person, not just a function. I respect you enough to greet you as a full human being.

He did not know, because nobody had taught him. Because the training he had received had prepared him for compliance, not for curiosity. For consistency, not for comprehension.

Because cultural intelligence was not yet part of the conversation.

Roberto, the HR manager, sat in that room and heard David's concern.

He was a calm man—steady in the way that people who have spent years managing human complexity in industrial environments learn to be steady. He had seen disputes and grievances and misunderstandings of every variety. He had learned to listen before he responded and to separate what was being said from what was actually happening.

He furrowed his brow.

"What do you mean?" he asked. "She kisses too much?"

There was no accusation in the question. It was genuine puzzlement—the specific puzzlement of a man from Reynosa, steeped in the same cultural norms as his colleague, trying to translate what he was hearing into something that made sense in the world he had grown up in.

David clarified. The cheek kisses. The greetings. The daily, constant, perfectly ordinary warmth that Roberto had never once thought to question because it was simply how things were done.

Roberto explained. This is normal here, he said. It is a professional greeting. It is how people show respect.

David listened. And did not shift.

And in that gap—between Roberto's explanation and David's unmoved position — the year of Magdalena's salary increase quietly disappeared.

I am back now. My voice, my perspective, my side of that conference room table.

I have spent a long time sitting with David's story. Not to forgive him—forgiveness is a personal matter and not the point of this chapter. Not to excuse what happened—the evaluation was real, the year was real, and the cost to me was real. But to understand him. Because understanding him is the only way to answer the question this book is actually asking.

How do we build something different?

The answer is not to find better Davids—people who are naturally more open, more curious, more culturally aware. There will always be Davids. There will always be people who have been formed by one cultural framework and who have not yet been given the tools to see past it. That is not a character flaw. It is the default condition of any human being who has not been taught to do otherwise.

The answer is to give people the tools. Before the evaluation. Before the policy. Before the four words get written down and the damage is done.

David needed someone to sit across from him—not in an HR training, not in a compliance module, not in a document he would sign and file—but in a real conversation, and ask him one question: When you watch her greet people that way, what do you feel? And where did that feeling come from?

Because the feeling was real. The discomfort was genuine. David was not performing concern. He was experiencing something that his cultural framework had no vocabulary for except wrong.

And if someone had helped him trace that feeling back to its source—to the particular culture and history and training that taught him what professional looked like—he might have arrived at a different question. Not: is this appropriate? But: appropriate according to whom? Whose definition of professional am I applying here? And is it possible that there is another valid definition operating in this room, one I have not yet learned to see?

That is Read. Applied to David. And the one I was many years ago that had tears in her eyes without understanding.

The same skill that I had to develop—to pause before my first interpretation became my only one, to ask whose framework I was using, to look for the other definition operating in the room—is the skill David needed and never received.

That is the tragedy of that conference room in Reynosa. Not that David was cruel. But that neither of us had been given the lens that would have made the conversation possible.

I want to pause here and point you toward something, because this moment in the book—this precise point of understanding that professional norms are cultural rather than universal—is where the academic world of cultural intelligence becomes genuinely useful.

Geert Hofstede, a Dutch social psychologist, spent decades researching how values in the workplace are influenced by culture. His framework identifies dimensions along which cultures differ—including how societies relate to hierarchy and power, how comfortable they are with uncertainty, how they balance individual achievement against collective belonging, and how they navigate the relationship between professional and personal life. If you had handed David a Hofstede cultural dimension chart before he flew to Reynosa, he would have found Mexico and the United States sitting in meaningfully different positions on nearly every dimension that governed the interaction he was about to misread.

Erin Meyer, in her book The Culture Map, offers a similarly practical framework — eight scales along which business cultures differ, from how directly people communicate to how they build trust to how they understand what a deadline actually means. Her work is precise, research-based, and deeply useful for anyone navigating the kind of cross-cultural professional environment David found himself in without a map.

I am not David's apologist. But I do believe in giving people tools rather than blame. Both Hofstede and Meyer offer tools that, in David's hands before that evaluation, might have produced a very different outcome. I encourage you to explore both—not as replacements for The Cultural Lens™, but as the kind of deeper cartography that makes the journey we are taking through this book richer and more precisely understood.

The map matters. David simply never had one.

I tell this story to leaders frequently. And the most common response I get—from the Magdalenas in the room—is recognition. A nod. Sometimes tears. The particular exhale of someone who has been carrying a story alone for years and has just heard it named.

The most common response I get from the Davids—from the managers and executives who hear themselves in his shoes—is something quieter. A stillness. The particular quality of attention that comes over someone who has just understood, for the first time, that they may have been David in someone else's story.

That recognition is not comfortable. I do not want it to be comfortable. But I want it to be survivable—something a person can sit with and then act from, rather than something so painful it becomes easier to look away.

Because the Davids who can sit with that recognition are the ones who change. Who go back to their teams and ask different questions. Who stop writing "she kisses too much" and start asking "what does this greeting mean to her?" Who build the kind of cultural intelligence that prevents the damage before it happens.

David, as far as I know, never changed. I do not know if anyone ever gave him the opportunity to.

But the leaders reading this book—the ones sitting with that quiet recognition right now—still have time.

Here is what I want to leave you with, from this chapter that has asked something unusual of both of us.

Read is not only the skill of understanding the people who are different from you. It is the skill of understanding the people who are like David—who are operating no idea that the standard they are applying is not neutral and never was.

Those people are not your enemies. They are the people who have not yet been taught to look. And in most organizations, most teams, most professional environments—they are also the people with the most power to change things, if someone gives them the framework to do it.

The question Read asks of you is this: can you see David clearly enough to help him see himself?

Not to excuse him. Not to carry his discomfort for him. But to hand him the lens he was never given—because that lens, in his hands, is the only thing that prevents the next Magdalena from leaving a conference room with tears in her eyes and a year of her career written off in four words.

She kisses too much.

He just didn't know what the kiss meant. That is the whole story. And the whole work.

✦

IF YOU WANT TO GO DEEPER

Two frameworks worth exploring alongside this chapter: Geert Hofstede's Cultural Dimensions Theory—available at hofstede-insights.com. Offers country comparison tools that show, in measurable terms, how cultures differ across power distance, individualism, uncertainty avoidance, and more.

Erin Meyer's The Culture Map (PublicAffairs, 2014). Eight scales. Precise, practical, and essential reading

Neither framework replaces the work of this book. Both deepen it.

A TOOL TO TAKE WITH YOU

The Lens Flip.

Think of a cross-cultural friction in your professional life—a misunderstanding, a conflict, a moment that felt wrong or was received badly.

Write the story once from your own perspective. What happened. What you felt. What you concluded.

Then write it again—from the other person's perspective. Use what you know about their cultural background, their professional context, their values and assumptions. What were they trying to do?

What did they believe they were communicating?

What standard were they applying—and where did it come from?

You do not have to agree with their version. You do not have to abandon yours.

You just have to hold both at the same time.

And its most powerful.

Because the moment you can see the room from two sides simultaneously, you stop being a participant in the misunderstanding.

You become the person who can resolve it.

✦

BRIDGE

"If you talk to a man in a language he understands, that goes to his head. If you talk to him in his language, that goes to his heart."
— *Nelson Mandela*

Chapter Nine

The Glass Door

The hallway was ordinary. That is the first thing I want you to know.

It was just a hallway—the kind that exists in every corporate office in every city in the world, fluorescent lights overhead, carpet chosen for durability rather than beauty, doors on either side leading to rooms where people were doing the ordinary work of an ordinary day. The kind of hallway you walk through a hundred times without remembering a single one.

I remember this one.

I was working for Motorola. My new American boss had met me that morning with the easy warmth of someone who makes people feel welcome without effort. He had given me a tour—the floor plan, the conference rooms, the kitchen where someone had left bagels out on a Tuesday for no reason anyone could explain. We talked as we walked, about the work and the team and what I was hoping to build there.

And then we reached a glass door.

He got there first. Without hesitation, without calculation, without any visible awareness that he was doing something worth noting—he reached out, pulled it open, and held it.

Waiting for me to walk through first.

◆

I stepped through the door.

And something cracked open in my chest.

Not dramatically. More quietly than that—the way ice cracks before it breaks, a sound so slight you almost miss it, but once you have heard it you know that something fundamental has shifted in the structure beneath.

I stood on the other side of that door and I thought, for the first time in longer than I could immediately calculate: When did I stop walking first?

◆

I have spent the better part of my career working inside Japanese corporate culture—not studying it, but living it, in the particular total way that happens when a workplace becomes the primary environment of your professional days. I still work in that world. I am writing this from inside it. And I mean what I say when I tell you that it is one of the most sophisticated systems of collective organization I have encountered in my life. The attention to craft. The depth of relational commitment. The way trust is built slowly and then held with a permanence that I find genuinely beautiful. I was shaped by my years inside it in ways I am still discovering. I cherish every single year of it.

And I also know, from the inside, exactly what it asked of me.

Hierarchy in Japanese professional culture moves through space the way it moves through language—naturally, visibly, as the simply correct order of things. Seniority leads. Those who are junior follow. In formal settings, in corridors, in the small choreography of bodies moving through a shared environment, position expresses itself physically. It is not aggressive or diminishing. It is how respect is communicated—how the organizational structure makes itself visible in daily life.

I had learned this. I had adapted to it, the way you adapt to anything that becomes the daily reality of your environment—gradually, incrementally, until the adaptation is complete and you no longer notice you are performing it.

At work, I had been walking behind for years.

I had not noticed until an American man held a door open and waited for me to go first, and the simple courtesy of it landed in my body like something I had almost forgotten was possible.

What this story is about is something precise and personal.

It is about what happens when adaptation becomes invisible to itself.

When you are adapting consciously—when you know what you are doing and why, when you can see the cultural gap you are crossing and you are choosing, deliberately, to meet the other person in their framework—that is Bridge. That is the skill this section of the book is about, and it is genuinely valuable and learnable.

When adaptation becomes unconscious—when the adjustments you made for one cultural environment have sedimented into habit, into default, into simply how you move through the world—something different has happened. You have not built a bridge. You have moved to the other shore and forgotten where you came from.

That is what the glass door revealed. Not that I had done anything wrong. But that I had been doing something so long, so automatically, so far below the level of conscious choice, that I had lost track of the woman who walked forward instead of behind.

Here is something I have observed across decades of working in multicultural environments that does not appear in most cultural intelligence frameworks, and that I want to name plainly.

The loudest cultural friction rarely comes from the cultures that are most visibly different from your own. It tends to come from the cultures that believe they have no culture—that their defaults are not defaults at all, but simply the correct way things should work. Cultures that have operated as the dominant frame in global business for long enough that they have mistaken their own norms for universal standards.

In that kind of environment, the expectation is not that the dominant culture will adapt. The expectation—often unstated, sometimes unconscious, but present and felt—is that everyone else will. That professionalism will be defined by one set of standards. That success will look a particular way. That the people who do not naturally fit that definition will learn to perform it well enough to pass.

In Europe, where geographic proximity has made multilingualism and cultural fluency a practical necessity for generations, there is a different baseline understanding—that navigating across cultures is simply what people do, that speaking several languages is ordinary rather than remarkable, that your colleague's different way of doing things is a feature of the landscape rather than a deviation from the norm.

I am not making an argument about which culture is correct. I am making an observation about which environments require cultural intelligence of everyone — and which environments require it only of some. Because that asymmetry matters. It matters to the people who are always doing the adapting. And it matters to the organizations that cannot see how much invisible labor is being performed in their hallways every single day.

◆

Bridge is the deliberate, conscious practice of meeting people where they are—adjusting your communication style, your pace, your approach—while keeping one hand on your own shore. It is genuine flexibility. It is one of the most sophisticated things a human being can learn to do.

Erasure is what happens when adaptation runs past its boundary. When you have adjusted so thoroughly, for so long, that the original—the you that walked in before the adjustments began—has become difficult to locate. When the flexibility has hardened into a new rigidity. When you are no longer choosing to adapt; you are simply operating from a self that has been quietly reshaped by the accumulated weight of all the rooms you have learned to fit inside.

The glass door did not tell me I had been wrong to adapt. It told me I had adapted past the point of choosing—and that somewhere along the way, the choosing had quietly stopped.

Bridge asks you to stay awake inside the adaptation. To keep one hand on your own shore even as you extend the other toward someone else's. To check in with yourself, regularly and honestly, to make sure the balance is still where you intended it to be.

✦

This is not only a personal story. I want to say that plainly before we go further.

When Bridge fails at scale—when an organization's culture requires certain people to do all the adapting, all the fitting, all the invisible labor of making themselves acceptable—the cost shows up in numbers that leadership can measure, if they choose to look. It shows up in turnover rates, disproportionately high among the employees who were doing the most adapting and receiving the least acknowledgment for it. It shows up in engagement scores—in the quiet withdrawal of people who have decided that showing up fully is not safe or rewarded. It shows up in innovation metrics, because the perspectives that were never fully welcomed are precisely the ones that would have generated the ideas the organization is now paying consultants to find.

And in environments where employment law takes seriously the obligation to create workplaces free from discrimination—where behavior that makes certain employees feel systematically invisible or undervalued can carry legal and financial consequences—the failure of Bridge is not only a cultural and human issue. It is a liability. Organizations that build cultural intelligence into their leadership development are not doing something nice. They are doing something necessary.

The woman walking behind in the hallway was not only losing something personal. The organization that normalized that dynamic was losing something too. It just did not know how to measure what it was losing, because it had never learned to see it.

After that hallway, I started walking first when I got there first.

It sounds small. It was the kind of small that accumulates into something significant—a daily, embodied reclamation of something I had ceded without quite meaning to. I walked through doors. I took up the space I was entitled to take up in rooms I had earned my place in. I adapted when adaptation served the work and the relationship—deliberately, skillfully, with full awareness of what I was doing and why. And when the adapting was done, I came back to myself.

Every time.

That return is Bridge. The going across and the coming back. The reach toward another shore and the knowledge of where your feet are standing while you reach.

That is what I had lost in the hallway, and what I reclaimed on the other side of the door.

I think about that hallway often. The ordinariness of it. The fluorescent lights and the unremarkable carpet and the glass door that my new boss held open without thinking about it, because in his cultural framework that was simply what you did.

He did not know what he was giving me.

He did not know that the woman who walked through that door first was, in some small but real way, more herself on the other side of it than she had been on the way in. That his unremarkable courtesy had cracked open a question that would take years to fully answer. That the hallway he would never remember was a hallway I would carry forward into every workshop and every keynote and every coaching conversation I have had since.

We teach what we needed to learn.

I teach Bridge because I know where its boundary is—from the inside, from years of experience on both sides of it. Because I found my way back, and I want to make sure you have a faster route than I did.

Walk through the door.

Walk through it first, when you get there first.

And check in with yourself—often, honestly—to make sure you still know the way back.

That is all Bridge asks.

A TOOL TO TAKE WITH YOU

The Identity Check.

After any significant professional adaptation — a new job, a new country, a new team, a long stretch inside a cultural environment that is not natively yours — sit with these three questions: One: What have I changed that I chose to change? (Adjustments made consciously, with open eyes, because they served the work or the relationship.)

Two: What have I changed that I did not choose? (Adaptations that happened gradually, below awareness, that you only noticed in retrospect—or not yet at all.)

Three: What am I still carrying that is unmistakably mine? (The things that have not shifted. The parts of yourself that remained through all the adaptation.

Name them. Hold them. They are your shore.)

The ones you chose, you can keep choosing.

The ones that happened to you—those deserve a second look.

That second look is Bridge.

Chapter Ten

What the Women in My Blood Knew

I was in my room in Strasbourg when I heard Elizabeth talking on the phone.

Elizabeth was my French host—the woman I had chosen to live with during the summer between semesters specifically because she spoke no English. I wanted total immersion. I wanted to be thrown into the deep end of the language with no lifeline, no comfortable retreat into something familiar. If I was going to learn French, I was going to learn it the way you learn things that matter: by having no other option.

I could hear her from down the hall—comfortable, unhurried, the easy cadence of someone having a perfectly ordinary conversation. I assumed it was a neighbor, a friend, someone from her world. I paid it no particular attention.

After a while, she appeared in my doorway. "Your mom wants to talk to you," she said. I stared at her.

My mom. You were speaking with my mom. In French.

⬤

I found out later what she had done. Not the outline of it—the actual, deliberate, months-long project of it.

My mother had enrolled in French language classes. She also took classes to use that new tool called email, unknown to her up until then, so she could practice and receive materials from her teachers. She had studied French phrases and customs and etiquette with the thoroughness of someone preparing for something important—learning enough about the culture to understand how to present herself to a French host, how to be warm without being intrusive, present without imposing.

She had done all of this quietly, without telling me, without asking for acknowledgment, without any fanfare at all.

She had done it so that when she needed to reach me, she could reach me on my terms. In the country I was living in. Through the woman who was watching over me in her absence.

She did not do it for a certificate. She did not do it for her career, or to impress anyone, or because someone told her she should. She did it for one reason and one reason only.

Connection.

The most purely motivated act of cultural intelligence I have ever witnessed in my life—and it was performed by my mother, in secret, in the years before I had a name for what she was doing.

Here is what I did not understand until much later, and what I want you to sit with now.

My mother lost her own mother when she was a little girl.

She grew up without the model that most of us take entirely for granted—the living, present example of what a mother does, how a mother stays close, what a mother reaches for when the person she loves is far away and the distance feels impossible. She did not have someone to watch and absorb and unconsciously replicate. She had to build it herself, from somewhere deeper than memory or imitation.

And what she built—the French classes, the emails, the preparation, the phone call to Elizabeth—was not something she had been taught. It was something she had decided. Something she had chosen, from the core of who she is, because she understood that love without effort is just a feeling, and that connection across distance requires something more than intention.

It requires action. Deliberate, humble, sometimes inconvenient action.

My mother built the bridge without a blueprint. She crossed the cultural and linguistic distance between Ramos Arizpe and Strasbourg one French vocabulary word at a time, because her daughter was on the other side and that was reason enough.

I was named María Magdalena after her. Before I ever understood the biblical meaning of my name, I saw what that name meant through her hands. She taught me that miracles are often hidden inside ordinary days—that prayer does not always sound like words, that a woman can carry a family on her shoulders and still dream with fire in her heart.

She is the cornerstone of my life. I dedicated The Modern Magdalena—a devotional for women navigating calling and responsibility—to her, carrying her name in its title because she is what that name means to me. She has faced her own challenges in these recent years, her sight almost taken from her, and she has met those challenges with the same quiet, unhurried determination she brought to those French lessons. We talk every day—from a quick good morning to an afternoon video call. My days feel like something is missing when we don't.

She asks about Mikel. She asks about my work. She is still, at her core, the woman who decided that no distance was too far to close.

She led herself the same way she crossed that distance—with intention and without drama. And that is what her proverb has always meant to me, lived out before I was old enough to understand it as wisdom: Para que los pollitos estén bien, la gallina debe estar buena.

For the chicks to be well, the hen must be well. A quiet instruction about the relationship between a leader's own wholeness and the wellbeing of everyone she is responsible for. My mother did not call it leadership. She called it being a mother. But the architecture is the same.

There is another photograph I have carried everywhere. It belongs to a different line of women—my father's—and to a different kind of strength entirely.

It is a photograph of my grandmother—Mami Mary, my father's mother. She is looking at the camera with the expression of a woman who has survived a great deal and arrived somewhere she did not expect. Beside her is a younger face—mine, at some celebration I can no longer precisely date, but whose feeling I remember clearly. The warmth of her. The solidity of her presence.

Mami Mary was taken from her parents' house when she was fourteen years old to be married. She was not consulted. She was not given options. The world she was born into had decided what her life would be before she had the chance to decide anything herself—not because the people around her were cruel, but because the culture they were living inside had not yet learned to imagine it differently.

She never went to school. She never had a birthday party as a little girl. She never had a doll.

She raised nine children.

And then, years later—when I was already in high school, when she was a grandmother of many, when most people in her generation had long since stopped imagining that new things were available to them—she enrolled in elementary school for adults. She sat in a classroom and she learned what she had been denied as a girl. She earned her own diploma.

My father brought her a doll.

All her children came together and gave her the birthday party she had never had — party hats and a piñata and the particular, enormous joy of a woman receiving something sixty years late and finding that it has lost none of its power to delight.

I keep her photograph where I can see it. Sometimes I talk to her. She is no longer with us. But she lives in us. I feel it in my bones.

◆

When I first decided to separate from Mikel's father, I went to Mami Mary.

I went with hesitation—with the particular combination of love and fear that you carry when you are about to say something to someone whose opinion matters more than you want it to. Someone from a generation and a culture where marriages lasted because that was simply what marriages did. I wanted to tell her before she heard it from someone else.

She listened to everything I said. And then she told me to just do it.

"You don't need to depend on a man to live your life and take care of your son," she said. Calm. Clear. Completely certain.

I was stunned. This was a woman who had been given to a man at fourteen and had built her entire life inside that arrangement—without complaint, with extraordinary grace. She had every reason, by the logic of her own experience, to counsel endurance. To say: stay. This is what women do.

She said the opposite. Because somewhere inside all of those years, all of that adaptation, all of that making-do and making-beautiful with what she had been handed, she had arrived at a clarity about what freedom actually meant—and she wanted it for me even if she had never had it for herself.

I am independent. An option she never had. I am educated, which was her goal.

I am raising my son in a country she could not have imagined, in a language she never spoke, building a life across cultural distances that would have seemed impossible from where she stood.

She watches over us. I believe this completely.

Three women. Three generations. Three expressions of the same intelligence—before any of us had a name for it.

Mami Mary, who adapted to every constraint her world placed on her and still found, in her seventies, the courage to want something new. Who gave her granddaughter permission she herself had never received. Who could not go further—and trusted me to go the rest of the way.

My mother, who lost her own mother as a little girl and still became one of the most naturally connected people I have ever known. Who learned French in secret so her daughter would never feel unreachable. Who leads herself first—para que los pollitos estén bien—so that everyone who depends on her can be well too.

And me—the one who finally had a word for what they were both doing. Who built a framework around the intelligence they lived instinctively. Who stands in front of rooms full of leaders and teaches what two women without degrees or frameworks or professional credentials had already understood: that connection across difference requires something active. That culture is not a wall. That the distance between two people, two languages, two worlds, is always crossable if someone is willing to do the work of crossing.

Bridge is not a professional skill I discovered in a training room. It is an inheritance. It was planted in me by women who had no vocabulary for it, who never read a book about cultural intelligence, who simply loved people across distances that could have made love impossible—and refused to let the distance win.

◆

I tell you their stories because I believe, with everything I have, that every reader of this book has a version of them in their own lineage.

Not necessarily a grandmother who earned a diploma at sixty. Not necessarily a mother who learned a foreign language in secret. But someone—somewhere in the family that made you, in the community that shaped you, in the particular human chain that leads back from where you are standing to where you came from—who crossed a cultural or linguistic or geographic distance for the sake of connection. Who adapted without erasing. Who built a bridge from scratch, without a blueprint, because someone they loved was on the other side.

That person is part of your Root. And their intelligence—the intelligence they practiced without naming it, the bridge they built without a framework—is already somewhere inside you.

Bridge, in the end, is not something you acquire. It is something you remember. Something that was modeled for you before you were old enough to take notes. Something that lives in the particular way you reach toward people, in the effort you are willing to make to stay connected, in the refusal to let distance—cultural, linguistic, geographic, generational—have the final word.

And when I stand in front of a room full of leaders—executives and HR directors and procurement managers and team leads, all of them trying to figure out how to navigate the cultural complexity of the organizations they are responsible for—I think about two women who never sat in a boardroom. Who never attended a leadership conference. Who never received a certificate in cross-cultural communication.

Who knew, anyway.

Who always knew.

My mother learned French so I would hear her voice.

Mami Mary learned to read so she could hold a diploma in her own name.

What did the women in your blood know—before they had a word for it?

◆

A TOOL TO TAKE WITH YOU

Who in your lineage built bridges before you did?

Think of someone—a parent, a grandparent, an aunt or uncle, a neighbor, a community member—who crossed a cultural, linguistic, or geographic distance for the sake of connection.

Who adapted without erasing.

Who stayed present across a gap that could have made presence impossible.

Write their name.

Then write one specific thing they did — one moment, one habit, one choice, one sacrifice—that you are still carrying forward today.

That is your inherited Bridge.

That is the intelligence that was in you before you ever opened this book.

Honor it.

Then build on it.

That is what they were hoping you would do.

Chapter Eleven

The Gift I Built in Someone Else's Language

Gifts are my love language.

Everyone who knows me understands this. It is how I express love and appreciation—through something chosen or made with care, something designed specifically for the person receiving it. It is also, not coincidentally, the instinct behind the small business I built to supplement my income as a solo parent: Opari Laser, where every personalized piece is created with intention, where every gift is meant to say something the giver cannot quite say any other way.

So it was perhaps inevitable that when I saw a need, I would respond to it the way I respond to most things that matter to me.

With a gift.

◆

A new president was arriving to lead our North American operations. I will call him Tanaka-san—a Japanese executive who would be landing in the United States to take responsibility for an organization of nearly five hundred people across four very different locations: a plant in Michigan, operations along the Texas-Mexico border, an engineering hub in Dallas, and a team in Los Angeles. Four cities. Four distinct cultures within the broader American context. Four sets of unspoken expectations about how leadership should look, how communication should flow, how trust gets built and what happens when it breaks.

He would be arriving from Japan. He would be managing in English, which was not his primary language. He would be stepping into a role that required him to understand—quickly, accurately, without the luxury of time to make gradual mistakes—the particular human landscape of each place he would be responsible for.

Nobody had prepared anything for him. I decided to.

Let me be honest about something before I describe what I built and why.

This was not my job. Nobody assigned it to me. Nobody asked me to do it, approved a budget for it, or even knew I was working on it until it was done. I was not in a senior leadership position. I was not his direct report, his assistant, his cultural liaison. I am a procurement professional with more than two decades of experience navigating the intersection of Japanese and American and Mexican business cultures—and I was watching a new leader prepare to walk into a situation that I recognized, from the inside, as genuinely complex.

I recognized it because I had lived it. Not as the executive arriving—but as the person already in the room when the executive arrived. I knew what it felt like to be on the receiving end of a leader who had not been given the tools to understand the environment they were walking into. I knew the friction that created—the misreads, the unintended slights, the trust that never quite built because the foundation was never properly laid.

And in my eyes, it was an act of kindness. A gift of something useful—more meaningful than a branded mug or logo apparel, more lasting than a welcome lunch. Because I knew what a well-prepared leader could do with the right information—how quickly relationships could form, how much damage could be prevented, how differently a team responds to someone who walks in having already done the work of understanding them.

So I built the guide.

◆

It was an abbreviated cultural compass—a document designed to give Tanaka-san the human landscape of the organization he was about to lead, in a language and a format that would be genuinely useful to him rather than to whoever happened to write it.

That distinction—genuinely useful to him rather than to whoever happened to write it—is the entire point of this chapter. It is also the most important thing I can teach you about Bridge.

Most welcome materials are written for the writer. They reflect the organization's self-image, its preferred talking points, the version of itself it wants the new person to receive. They are written in the register and format that the existing culture is comfortable with. They assume the new leader will adapt to them.

I wrote in the opposite direction.

I thought about Tanaka-san. What he was coming from—the precision and hierarchy of Japanese corporate culture, the particular way trust is built there, the communication styles he was accustomed to, what respect looked like in his world. What he would be walking into—the directness of American professional culture, the informality, the egalitarian expectations, the different rhythms of each of our four locations. What he would need to understand, as quickly as possible, to lead effectively without the kind of early mistakes that damage relationships before they have a chance to form.

And I wrote for him. In his frame. On his terms.

The guide was bilingual—English and Japanese, side by side, so that the most important information was available in his first language and he did not have to work harder than necessary to access it. It covered the regional culture of each location: the working-class pride and technical precision of Michigan, the community-oriented warmth and relationship-first culture of the Texas-Mexico border, the business-driven professionalism of Dallas, the creative energy and informality of Los Angeles. It covered American workplace norms—the direct communication, the expectations around punctuality and accessibility, the particular way Americans read leadership—explained not as criticism of Japanese culture but as context for what he would encounter.

It covered practical things: how meetings typically run, what small talk sounds like and why it matters, how business cards are exchanged, how to read eye contact and personal space and the particular social choreography of an American office.

And it ended with a line I still believe with everything I have: Leadership is about building bridges across cultures.

I presented it to him before he officially took his role.

He sat with it for a long moment. Longer than I expected. He turned pages carefully—the way you handle something that has been made with care, with the particular attention of someone who recognizes effort and does not rush past it. He read sections in Japanese. He looked at the regional maps.

And then he looked at me.

What passed between us in that moment did not require translation. There was no equivalent in either of our languages for the specific thing that happened—the recognition, across a significant cultural distance, that someone had seen you clearly enough to prepare for your arrival. That someone had done the work of understanding your world before they asked you to understand theirs.

It was not gratitude, exactly. It was something more structural than gratitude—the laying of a foundation. The beginning of a trust that would not have to be earned from scratch, because the first act of the relationship had already been an act of genuine understanding.

He thanked me. I bowed slightly—the particular, almost-unconscious muscle memory of twenty years of Japanese professional culture, the body doing what it had learned even when the mind had moved on.

He noticed. And he smiled. That smile, and everything it carried, was worth every hour I had spent building it.

I want to pull back for a moment and name what was actually happening in the making of that guide, because it was a precise application of everything Bridge requires.

ROOT first. I knew what I was carrying into that project—my years inside Japanese corporate culture, my understanding of what a new leader from that world would find familiar and what would be genuinely foreign, my experience of being the person in the room who navigated between multiple cultural frameworks every day. I was not guessing about Tanaka-san's world. I was drawing on two decades of firsthand knowledge of it.

READ second. Before I wrote a single word, I thought carefully about what he would need to know—not what I would want to tell him, not what the organization was comfortable sharing, but what he, specifically, coming from where he was coming from, would need to understand to lead well from his very first day. I read the situation from inside his frame, not mine.

And then BRIDGE. The actual act of building—of taking what I knew about both worlds and constructing something that could carry a person safely from one to the other. Not a document that asked him to figure out how to be American. A document that met him exactly where he was and walked with him into the landscape he was about to navigate.

Bridge does not say: come be like me. Bridge says: let me understand where you are and then let me build something that reaches from there to here. Let me do the work of crossing first, so that when we meet in the middle, we are meeting on ground that was built for both of us.

The guide I built for Tanaka-san was not a complicated thing. It did not require a large budget or a specialized team or months of preparation. It required attention, knowledge, and the decision to use both in service of someone else's success rather than my own comfort.

And here is what I want you to understand clearly: that guide—that precise act of cultural translation, offered as a gift before anyone asked for it—is now one of the highest-value services Cultural Intelligence Solutions offers. The Expatriate Cultural Guide™ is a product built on that exact experience. A custom, bilingual cultural compass for incoming international executives, designed to give them the human landscape of the organization and region they are about to lead—before they arrive, before the first misread happens, before trust has to be repaired instead of built.

I did not set out to build a business product that day. I set out to offer a thoughtful gift to a man who was walking into a complex situation unequipped with cultural intelligence. But what I discovered in the making of it was that the need is universal. Every Japanese executive arriving to lead a US operation needs this. Every German engineer taking over a Mexican plant needs this. Every American executive landing in Seoul or Singapore or São Paulo without a cultural map needs this.

The gap between what organizations provide and what leaders actually need to succeed across cultural lines is enormous. And the cost of that gap—in friction, in damaged relationships, in turnover, in deals that never quite close—is measurable, even when it is rarely measured.

That single act of kindness became a product. The product became a business. The business became part of a framework that I now teach to organizations and leaders around the world.

Gifts, it turns out, are my professional language too.

I learned something from building that guide that I could not have learned any other way.

I learned that Bridge, at its best, does not feel like a skill you are deploying. It feels like clarity—the particular clarity of a person who knows two worlds well enough to move between them fluidly, who can stand on one shore and describe the other with accuracy and warmth and the specific kind of respect that comes from genuine knowledge rather than assumption.

I had spent twenty years accumulating that clarity without quite knowing that was what I was doing. Every negotiation across cultural lines, every misunderstanding navigated, every meeting where I was reading two cultural frameworks simultaneously and finding the language that could work in both—all of it had been preparation for a moment like that one. For the ability to sit down and write, in two languages, a map of a landscape I had spent my career learning to navigate.

The guide was a gift to him. But so was the making of it—to me, as much as to anyone. Because it was the moment I understood, for the first time clearly, what I had actually been building across all those years.

Not just a career. Not just expertise in procurement and supply chain and cross-cultural negotiation.

A bridge.

One that had been under construction my entire professional life, built from both shores simultaneously, and that was ready—finally, precisely, in that moment—to carry someone across.

Think about who, in your organization right now, is about to arrive without a map.

A new leader from another country. A team member relocating across a cultural boundary. A supplier from a business culture your organization has never worked with before. Someone who is about to walk into a landscape that everyone around them has spent years learning to navigate—and who will have to figure it out alone, through trial and error and the particular, avoidable cost of early misreads.

You know things they do not know yet. You understand this environment in ways they will have to discover on their own—unless someone offers to show them.

That offering is Bridge. And it does not have to be a bilingual document. It can be a conversation. A lunch. A walk through the office with the kind of honest, specific, culturally informed commentary that no onboarding packet ever contains. The things you would want someone to tell you, offered freely to the person who needs them.

Build the guide. In someone else's language.

Before they arrive. Before they ask. Before it becomes necessary.

Because in Bridge, the most important moment is always the one before the meeting.

A TOOL TO TAKE WITH YOU

The Bridge Builder Preparation.

Before your next important cross-cultural meeting, negotiation, on-boarding, or relationship — spend twenty minutes with these questions: One: What do I know about this person's cultural world that they may not expect me to know?

(Their communication style, their definition of respect, how hierarchy functions in their professional culture, what trust looks like and how it is built.)

Two: What do they need to understand about my world that no one may have thought to tell them?

(The unspoken rules, the cultural defaults, the things everyone here knows and no one explains.)

Three: What can I offer—before we meet — that would make the crossing easier for both of us? (A conversation, a document, a lunch, an honest walk through the landscape they are about to enter.)

The most important moment in Bridge is always the one before the meeting. Prepare for it.

◆

RISE

"We rise by lifting others."
— *Robert Ingersoll*

Chapter Twelve

We Build the Table Ourselves

The alarm goes off at 4:45 in the morning.

Not because anyone has to be at an office by five. Not because a flight is leaving or a deadline has arrived. But because a group of women has decided—collectively, deliberately, by mutual agreement—that this hour belongs to them. To accountability. To the specific, sometimes uncomfortable, always generative work of holding each other to the standard of who they said they wanted to become.

The M3 Mastermind meets at five AM on Wednesdays. It has been meeting that way for almost three years.

M3 was Giselle's vision. She saw the need before the rest of us had named it—the specific kind of intentional, high-accountability sisterhood that most professional women want and almost none of us have. She invited us in. We said yes. And then we built it together, one Wednesday morning at a time.

We set the alarm. We show up. Every week. Even when it is hard. Especially when it is hard.

That is Rise. In its simplest, most essential form.

The women of M3 are not interchangeable. Each one brings something distinct—a perspective, a discipline, a way of seeing that the group would be smaller without.

Giselle, who founded us, leads with vision and an almost alarming clarity about where she is going and why. Eliza, whose faith and commitment to showing up is the kind that makes everyone around her rethink their excuses. Caro, who gives feedback with the precision of someone who respects you too much to be soft about it. Queen Esther, who brings the kind of focus to goal-setting that turns good intentions into actual results. Marie, who holds space for the emotional truth of the work in a way that keeps us honest about what is really happening beneath the surface of our professional lives.

Together we have built something that none of us could have built alone: the upper room where the real conversations happen. A covenant where someone can say I am stuck, or I am afraid, or I do not know how to ask for what I need—and be met with both compassion and accountability. Where the wins are celebrated genuinely, the setbacks are processed without judgment, and the standard is always: above all we lead with love and understanding, we Rise.

I hosted Episode 7 of our podcast: Celebrating Wins. You can find it on Spotify, and I cordially invite you to listen.

The topic sounds simple but is not, specially for women who have been taught—by culture, by family, by the particular social conditioning that tells us that celebrating ourselves is arrogance—the practice of acknowledging how far we have come is genuinely countercultural. We have been shaped to minimize. To deflect. To say it was nothing, it was luck, it was everyone else. The episode I led asked us to do the opposite. To name the win. To sit in it. To say: I did this, and it mattered, and I am allowed to know it.

That practice sounds small. It is, in fact, one of the most radical things a woman can do.

Rise is not only about building environments for other people. It is also about building them for yourself. About creating the conditions in which your own growth can happen—not waiting for someone to notice your potential and offer you the room, but walking into your own life with both hands and making the room yourself.

M3 is that room. Built at five in the morning, by women who decided that the table they needed was not going to appear on its own.

Some of the most important relationships in a life begin in the most ordinary moments.

I met Cris at a local faith radio station—both of us volunteering one morning for reasons that had nothing to do with each other and everything to do with who we each were. We started talking. Something in the conversation told me immediately that this was a woman with layers. I was right.

Cristina Solis Wilson is a decorated Command Sergeant Major with more than twenty-six years of U.S. Army Reserve service, a combat veteran, a published author, an international speaker, a certified John Maxwell coach, and the Chief Strategy Officer of the Entrepreneur Power Network. She has been named Business Woman of the Year and Women of Influence by SUCCESS Magazine. She chairs organizations, co-founds initiatives, and shows up in the kind of community work that never makes the highlight reel but always makes the difference.

She is also the woman who opened a Cub Scout chapter for Mikel and her nephew. Not because it was convenient. Not because her own children needed it. Because two boys needed it and she was the person who could make it happen.

That detail tells you everything about who Cris is. She does not Rise by accumulating titles—though she has earned every one of them. She Rises by building tables for the people around her, regardless of whether there is anything in it for her except the knowledge that she showed up.

She is my accountability partner within EPN, and she and her husband Mike are local family—present not for the events but for the ordinary texture of a life shared across years. To be in her orbit is to be held to a standard. She embodies what she teaches: that excellence is a journey, not a destination.

I could keep going. I want to keep going. The women who have shaped me are too many to name in one chapter—Roxana, who built a life across cultures with the ease of someone born to belong everywhere. The members of HWNT-RGV, where I have watched Latina professionals step into their leadership one courageous act at a time. Perla and The Latina Empire community, where women from across the hemisphere show up before the world is awake to do the work of becoming who they were always meant to be. To my best friend Norma, to Emma, Karla, Sarah, Marsha, Elizabeth, Deborah, to Sabrina and so many many more I wish I could list right here.

There is a principle I believe with everything I am, and that the research consistently confirms: you become a reflection of the people you surround yourself with. Not because you lose yourself in them—but because the standards, habits, and ways of seeing the world that exist in your close community become the water you swim in. The invisible environment that shapes your default assumptions about what is possible, what is expected, and what you owe to yourself and to others.

This is why Rise is not a solo act. It never has been.

The most capable, most accomplished, most culturally intelligent leaders I know did not become that way in isolation. They became that way because at some essential point in their journey, they were surrounded by people who held a higher standard. Who reflected back to them a version of themselves that was larger than what they had previously imagined. Who refused, by their own example and by the quiet expectation of their presence, to let them settle for the smaller life.

If you do not have that community yet, building it is the most important work you can do. Not networking—community. The difference is intention. Networking is transactional: what can we exchange? Community is relational: who are we becoming together?

Rise builds tables. But it also chooses chairs—carefully, deliberately, with full awareness that the people sitting at them will shape the person you are becoming.

◆

I want to talk about what happens when you try to build the table inside a system that is not sure it wants one.

I have seen this pattern more than once—in my own experience and in the organizations I have worked alongside. Someone inside a large institution sees a need. A gap in how people are being developed, supported, or prepared for the complexity of the environment they work in. They design something. They name it with care. They build the case, present the proposal, navigate the institutional review process—the budget questions, the scope concerns, the competing priorities, the particular caution of systems that move slowly even when the need moves fast.

Sometimes the initiative launches and runs beautifully. Sometimes it gets reduced to something smaller than what was proposed. Sometimes it gets cancelled before it finds its footing. And sometimes the person who built it is told — explicitly or implicitly—that this kind of work is not their lane. That someone else owns this. That the timing is not right.

And sometimes that person keeps showing up anyway.

Not loudly. Not with ultimatums or the exhausting energy of someone who has turned their cause into everyone else's burden. Quietly. With the patient, clear-eyed persistence of someone who knows that the work matters even when the institution has not yet caught up to why.

What I have learned—from watching this pattern, from living it—is that a cancelled program is not a cancelled impact. The relationships built inside it survive the cancellation. The conversations started do not un-start themselves. The person who walked into that initiative and left with a different question than the one they arrived with does not lose that question when the program ends.

The institution may not know how to measure what was built. But something was built.

Rise does not require institutional endorsement. It requires the willingness to start—and then to keep starting, with the same conviction and the same care, even when the system around you has not yet decided to keep up.

Three expressions of Rise. One truth at the center of all of them.

Rise is not the destination. It is not the title, the award, the program successfully institutionalized, the mastermind group that runs perfectly every week. Rise is the direction—the consistent, deliberate orientation toward something larger than your current comfort, pursued in community with people who hold you to it.

The alarm at 4:45 is Rise. The woman who opens a Cub Scout chapter because two boys need one is Rise. The professional who keeps proposing the initiative after it has been reduced, who keeps showing up with the conviction that the work matters even when the system has not yet agreed—that is Rise.

And you are the reflection of the people you do it with.

So choose your people with the same care you give to your vision. Build the table with intention. Set the alarm with commitment. Keep showing up—for the work, for the community, for the version of yourself that is still being built.

That version is waiting for you at five AM on a Wednesday. And at every table you have not yet built.

✦

A TOOL TO TAKE WITH YOU

The Rise Circle.

Who are the three to five people in your life who hold you to a higher standard than you hold yourself?

Who challenges you—warmly, honestly, with genuine investment in who you are becoming?

Who celebrates your wins without envy and names your blind spots without judgment?

Write their names.

If you cannot name three to five people who fit that description, that is your most important piece of information.

Then ask: what table do I need that does not yet exist? What community am I waiting for someone else to build that I could build myself?

Rise builds tables.

And it always begins with someone willing to set the first chair.

You are allowed to be that person. You may already be that person.

The question is whether you are willing to start.

Chapter Thirteen

A testimony in 4 words—The Lens Is Yours Now

I stood in front of a room full of young Latinas and asked them to do something unusual.

Place your hand over your heart. Feel it beating. Understand that the blood moving through you came from somewhere—from people who sacrificed things you will never fully know so that you could be standing in this room, in this moment, with this possibility in front of you.

Then I asked them: what does that heartbeat is carrying within your veins? Courage? resilience? Strength? Fear? Faith?

I drove home that evening the way I always do after I speak—in the particular quiet that follows a session where something real happened in the room.

Replaying moments. Wondering which ones landed. Carrying the low-grade uncertainty of a person who put something genuine into the world and does not yet know how it was received.

Months later, I found out.

◆

A student from that session wrote an essay for a scholarship application. She was applying through the Hispanic Women's Network of Texas, RGV chapter—the same organization I have been part of for years, the same community that has held and challenged and developed so many of the Latinas in our region. The essay prompt asked her to write about a significant experience from the program that had impacted her most.

She wrote about my session.

She described growing up in a bilingual household where English was the language of school and Spanish was the language of family—and how, somewhere in the navigation between those two worlds, the Spanish had gotten quieter. How she had sat across from her great-grandmothers, wanting to ask them about their lives, about the traditions that lived in their hands and their kitchens and their stories, and not having the words to reach them. How she had lost both great-grandmothers in the same year, carrying a grief that was not only for the women themselves but for the conversations that had never happened.

She wrote about the moment in my session when I asked the room to place their hands over their hearts. She wrote that she understood, in that moment, that she was there because of them—because of the people whose heartbeat she carried, whose sacrifices had made her room possible. She wrote that what had felt like a deficiency—not speaking Spanish, not knowing the traditions, not being able to connect across the language her family brought from another place and another time—she now saw as an opportunity still available to her.

Then she described what she did after she went home.

She asked her parents to teach her Spanish. She committed to learning one new word every day. And when she had learned enough—when she had built enough vocabulary to hold the sentence in her mouth—she walked up to her grandmother and said, for the first time in her life, the first complete sentence she had ever spoken to her in Spanish: Te quiero mucho, abuela.

Her grandmother smiled.

She wrote: I felt as though I had finally returned home. Her grandmother passed shortly after.

She also wrote that after the session, she joined her school's Student Council. That by the end of her junior year she had been elected Junior Class President. That she now serves as Senior Senator. That the session had given her the confidence to speak—and that she has been speaking ever since.

I read that essay and I sat with it for a long time.

Not because it confirmed something I had hoped for. But because it showed me something I had not fully understood about what this work actually is.

I did not teach her to love her grandmother.

I did not teach her resilience, or the courage to run for class president, or the hunger to reconnect with the language her family carried across generations. Those things were already in her. They were in her blood, in the heartbeat she had been carrying her entire life without fully understanding where it came from or what it was asking of her.

What I offered was a moment. A hand over a heart. A question about what they are bringing with them from the people who came before and the people who will come after. A framework that gave her a way to understand what she was already feeling—and a language for what she was already, instinctively, reaching toward.

That is all The Cultural Lens™ has ever been.

Not a replacement for what you already carry. Not a system that teaches you who to be. A lens—a way of seeing more clearly what is already present in you, so that you can use it deliberately, bring it forward consciously, and offer it to the world with the full weight of everything it actually contains.

The student did not need me to tell her that her culture mattered. She needed a moment that made it possible for her to remember what she already knew.

You do not need this book to tell you who you are.

You need it to help you see what you have been carrying all along. And by doing so, having the understanding that each person in front of you has their own lenses too.

We have traveled a long way together in these pages. Through boardrooms in Indiana and lecture halls in Grenoble and hallways in New York and conference rooms in Reynosa. Through kitchens in Saltillo and radio stations in McAllen and early Wednesday mornings that belong to women who decided not to wait.

Through the stories of women taken at fourteen and given to marriages they did not choose, who still found ways to hand their granddaughters the freedoms they themselves were never offered.

All of it—every story, every moment of friction and clarity and recognition—has been pointing toward the same four things.

Root — Recognize what you carry. Before you walk into any room, any negotiation, any relationship across difference, understand the lens you are already looking through. Know what your culture taught you about authority, time, silence, conflict, success, and belonging. Know what it gave you and what it cost you.

Know where you are standing when you reach toward someone else's shore.

Read — See the room as it actually is. Pause before your first interpretation becomes your only one. Ask whose cultural framework you are using to read what you are seeing. Look for the other definition of professionalism, of respect, of warmth, of trust that may be operating in the room—the one that belongs to the person in front of you rather than the one you brought in. Hold both lenses at once, and let what you see surprise you.

Bridge — Connect without disappearing. Meet people where they are—in their frame, on their terms, with genuine understanding of what their world requires.

Adjust your communication, your pace, your approach. And while you do, keep one hand on your own shore. Know what you are choosing to adapt and what you are choosing to keep. Check in with yourself often enough that the adaptation stays conscious and the original stays intact.

Rise — Lead so others can too. Build the environments, the communities, the tables that make it possible for the people around you to do what you have learned to do. Not to perform generosity, not to accumulate followers, but because you know—from the inside, from the cost of doing it without support—what a difference it makes when someone holds the door open before you even know to ask.

These four pillars are not a checklist. You do not complete them in order and arrive somewhere finished. They are a practice—a daily, lifelong, always-deepening set of questions that you bring to every room you enter, every relationship you build, every moment of cultural difference that asks something of you.

The question at the center of all of them—the one that started in that conference room in Reynosa and has not stopped working since—is still the most important one I know: Is this bias? Is this fear?

Or is this my cultural subconscious—and am I willing to see past it?

Ask it before you react. Ask it before you judge. Ask it before four words end up in someone's official record, or a relationship closes before it opens, or a room loses the contribution of someone who did not feel safe enough to offer it.

The lens does not answer the question for you. It teaches you to ask it. And asking it—consistently, honestly, in the rooms where it is hardest—is the whole practice.

This book is the beginning of a conversation, not the end of one.

If something in these pages cracked open a question you want to keep exploring — if you put your hand over your heart at some point in the reading and felt the weight of what you are carrying and the possibility of what you could do with it—I want to make sure you know where the conversation continues.

WHERE WE GO FROM HERE

The Cultural Lens™ Pulse Check—free.

Take the assessment at [www.culturalintelligencesolutions.com]. Discover your profile.

Find out where you are in the framework—and where your next step lives.

Cultural Decode™—the podcast.

Every episode decodes one cultural moment.

Real voices. Real stories. The conversation that this book started, continuing. Find it wherever you listen to podcasts.

The Cultural Lens™ Online Course—go deeper.

Four modules. One per pillar. Magdalena as your guide.

For the person who wants more than insight—who wants practice.

The Cultural Lens™ for Teams—bring it to your organization. Workshops, consulting, the Expatriate Cultural Guide™.

For leaders who are ready to build the room.

Find all of it at [www.culturalintelligencesolutions.com] · \@thecq-coach on Instagram and LinkedIn.

Before you close this book, I want to ask you to do one thing. Not a quiz. Not an assessment. Not another framework exercise. A declaration.

The student who went home from my session and learned Spanish one word at a time was not waiting for permission. She was not waiting until she felt ready or qualified or sufficiently prepared. She was not waiting for the room to tell her that her culture was welcome in it. She decided—quietly, on her own, in the ordinary privacy of a life that no one was watching—that the distance between who she was and who she wanted to be was crossable. And then she started crossing it.

That is Rise. In its most essential, most personal, most irreducible form.

You have read about Root and Read and Bridge. You have met the women who lived these pillars before they had names—the grandmother who earned her diploma at sixty, the mother who learned French in secret, the woman who set an alarm at 4:45 in the morning because she decided this hour belonged to her development. You have seen what cultural intelligence looks like when it is practiced in the body, in the family, in the hallway, in the guide built in someone else's language for someone who has not yet arrived.

Now it is your turn.

YOUR RISE DECLARATION

Write one paragraph. Sign it. Keep it.

What kind of room are you building? Who are you building it for?

What will be different—for the people who come after you, for the teams you lead, for the communities you belong to—because you showed up fully, today, as exactly who you are?

Do not write what sounds good. Write what is true.

That paragraph is your Rise Declaration.

It is the promise you make—not to anyone else, but to yourself and to the people whose heartbeat you are carrying forward.

Sign it. Date it.

Put it somewhere you will find it on a hard day.

Then go build the room.

I do not know which room you are standing in right now.

I do not know what you are navigating—what cultures are present in your professional life, what distances you are trying to cross, what the cost has been of doing this work without a framework, or what it might mean for you to have one now.

What I know is that you picked up this book. That something in you said: I need to understand this. Or: I need language for what I am already living. Or: I need proof that the thing I have been doing intuitively—the bridge I have been building without a name for it—has value and method and a place in the professional world.

That reaching—whatever form it took for you—is the awakening.

It started before page one. It started the moment you recognized something in the title, or the back cover, or the description that said: this is about something I know. Something I have been inside of, navigating without a map.

The map is yours now. Root. Read. Bridge. Rise. The lens is yours.

And to every reader who has made it to this page—to the Sofias who have been told to make themselves smaller, and to the Davids who did not yet know what they were missing, and to everyone who has stood in a room that was not built for them and stayed anyway:

See the world differently. Lead it boldly.

Epilogue

The Cultural Awakening Is Not an Event. It Is a Practice.

I want to tell you where I am as I write these final pages.

I am in the Rio Grande Valley—on the border between two countries, in a city that has always understood, out of geographic necessity, that navigating between cultures is not a special skill. It is simply how life works here. The people I grew up around have been code-switching since before there was a word for it. They have been building bridges between languages and customs and ways of seeing the world since long before anyone offered them a framework for it.

I grew up here too, eventually. Though I arrived the long way—through Toluca and Saltillo and Grenoble and Detroit and Tokyo and the particular, circuitous route that life takes when it is shaping you for something you cannot yet name.

I am fifty-one years old. I have been navigating multicultural environments for more than three decades. And I am still learning.

I want you to know that before you put this book down, because the most important thing I can leave you with is not a framework or a tool or a declaration — though all of those matter. It is this: The awakening does not end.

I still catch myself in the old patterns. Still notice, sometimes, that I have been walking behind when I arrived first. Still feel the impulse, in certain rooms with certain people, to make myself a little smaller—to quiet the accent or soften the directness or leave the greeting on the other side of the door where no one can read it incorrectly. Or to respond from the gut not the brain.

The difference now is that I notice it. And noticing it, I have a choice.

That choice—the moment between the old pattern and the conscious response—is the entire practice. It does not always feel like a moment of cultural intelligence. Sometimes it feels like a breath. A pause. A small internal question that most people in the room would never see. But it is there, and it is mine, and it was built across thirty years of navigating rooms that were not always built for me.

The Cultural Lens™ did not give me that choice. Experience gave it to me. What the framework gave me was the language to teach it—to take something I had been doing by instinct and survival and make it accessible to people who have not yet had thirty years to figure it out on their own.

That is the whole project. That is why this book exists.

I think about the girl from Toluca sometimes. The one who wanted to be a flight attendant—who wanted, underneath the uniform and the cart and the practiced calm in turbulence, to see the world. Whose father said think bigger, and who did — who dreamed of being an ambassador and then watched that dream get redirected by love and by culture and by the particular walls that existed around the ambitions of young women in the Mexico she grew up in.

She would not recognize my life. Not because it is extraordinary—though it has been full, and difficult, and rich in the specific way that lives built across borders tend to be. But because the world she was standing in when she spread that city map on the table and found the farthest school had no room in it for what she would eventually become.

The CQ Coach. The author. The speaker. The founder. The mother who raised a son with a blindfold and a world map and the absolute conviction that the world was worth understanding.

None of that was visible from Saltillo.

All of it was being built.

That is the other thing I want to leave you with—the companion truth to the one about the practice never ending. The path you are on is building something you cannot yet see. The rooms you are navigating now, the cultural distances you are crossing without a map, the moments of friction and misread and hard-won clarity—they are not obstacles to the work. They are the work. They are what you will eventually teach, if you choose to.

A book is never written alone. This one less than most.

It was written from the stories of my father, who left Torreón at twenty and studied English at the kitchen table at night so his children could have more doors. From my mother, who learned French in secret so her daughter would never feel unreachable. From Mami Mary, who was given no choices and still found a way to hand her granddaughters the freedom she never had.

It was written from the women of M3, who set an alarm and showed up at 5AM. From Cristina, who opened a Cub Scout chapter because two boys needed one. From Roxana, who stayed in France and built a life that was always going to belong everywhere. From every woman in the HWNT-RGV and Latina Empire communities who showed up, year after year, for the specific, essential work of lifting each other.

It was written from the student who went home from one of my sessions and learned to say te quiero mucho to her grandmother. She does not know this book exists yet. When she reads it, I hope she understands what her essay gave me—proof, at the exact moment I needed it, that the work was real.

And it was written from Mikel. Who challenged me to put my phone down on Sundays. Who pointed at the map with his eyes closed and taught me, by being curious about everywhere his finger landed, that cultural intelligence is not a professional skill. It is a way of being in the world. It can be built into the rhythms of an ordinary life. It can be passed forward.

He is eighteen now. He is heading to UTRGV in the fall, and then—if the dream holds—to Paris, to Le Cordon Bleu, to the city where Roxana lives and where Alejandro has promised to take him out for a drink the moment he arrives. He will carry the map with him. The blindfold too, in the best sense—the willingness to land somewhere unfamiliar and decide it is worth understanding.

He is my greatest work. And he is entirely his own.

The cultural awakening is not an event. It does not happen once, in a conference room or a lecture hall or a chapter of a book, and then settle into a permanent state of achieved understanding.

It is a practice. Daily, imperfect, ongoing. A set of questions you bring to every new room, every unfamiliar culture, every moment of difference that asks something of you. A willingness to keep looking, even when—especially when—what you see is yourself.

The lens is not a destination. It is the way you travel.

◆

Root. Read. Bridge. Rise.

Every day. In every room. With every person who is navigating a world that was not built for them—and with every person who has the power to build it differently.

See the world differently.

Lead it boldly.

Con todo mi cariño y respeto,

Magdalena Aguinaga
The CQ Coach Mission, Texas

Cultural Ambassadors

This book exists because a community believed in it before it was published.

The following individuals and organizations answered the call to become Cultural Ambassadors—investing not only in these pages but in the mission behind them: that cultural intelligence is not a luxury, not a corporate initiative, and not someone else's responsibility. It is the work of every person willing to see the world through a wider lens.

To each Ambassador: your name lives in every copy of this book, in every room it enters, and in every conversation it starts. Thank you for building this with me.

Inclusive·Beautiful·Delicious.

Continue the conversation.

Scan to visit Magdalena's Amazon Author Page—find all her published works, follow for new releases, and leave a review for The Cultural Awakening™. Your review matters more than you know. It is how the next reader finds this book.

See the world differently. Lead it boldly.

To know more about Magdalena's work visit:
www.culturalintelligencesolution.com